PRAISE FOR 1-2-3 MAGIC

What parents are saying:

"This book **changed our lives**."

"My three-year-old has become a different little girl, **and she is so much happier now**."

"**The ideas in this book work!** It really is like magic! I feel like **I am back in charge**."

"Simple, clear, concise, and **easy to follow**."

"**I highly recommend this book** if you need a method of dealing with your little one(s) that keeps everyone calm."

"Extremely **helpful and informative**."

"A **great book** for any parent!"

"**I was desperate for a change** in my family dynamics. **This book was the answer!**"

"**Fantastic book** that really helps with toddler tantrums. **My husband and I both read it** and now **we are disciplining in the same way**. This book has been a **lifesaver!**"

"*1-2-3 Magic* **simplifies everything** I've read in other books, which makes it **very easy to follow**. Our home has become **a much more positive place**."

"**Easy to read** and easy to follow."

"**Buy this book; read this book; follow the instructions in this book!** I highly recommend this to anyone involved in disciplining children."

"*1-2-3 Magic* **made parenting fun again.**"

"All I have to say is that **the ideas in this book WORK!** It really is like magic!"

"**This book is amazing!** My three-year-old was having major tantrums 4-6 times a day, screaming at the top of his lungs. After applying *1-2-3 Magic*, he rarely has meltdowns."

"*1-2-3 Magic* **takes the stress out of discipline.**"

"**It's such a relief to not feel like I'm constantly yelling at someone!** If you want to see a fast improvement in your child's behavior, check out *1-2-3 Magic*."

"Fantastic book that **really helps with my toddler's tantrums.**"

"This is the **one-stop, go-to book** that we have referred to time and again."

"This book is a great tool! It **helped me feel confident and proud of my parenting skills**."

"The methods are described clearly and they are **easy for any parent to follow**. I am **already seeing an improvement** in the way I react to my five- and seven-year-olds."

"We feel **more in charge** and **in control**."

"**Saved my blood pressure** and my relationship with my kids."

"**This book isn't just about time-outs and discipline**; it encompasses an entire parenting philosophy."

"**I highly recommend this book** to any parent who is s**pending more time yelling at or nagging** their children **than smiling at and laughing with them**."

"**Thank you**, Dr. Phelan, for **sharing the results of your extensive research** and experimentation with the rest of the world!"

"*1-2-3 Magic* **saved my marriage**."

"This is a **must-read** for all parents."

"Our little girl had gotten full-blown into the terrible twos and **I was desperate to get the calm back in my household**. She caught on to this method in one day. **Our house is a pleasant place to be again**."

"This book **really helps!**"

"If you have challenges with your kids and you consistently follow the directions in this book, **you will have such a better relationship with your children**."

"I have read many discipline books and tried many different methods. **This was the one that worked for our family**."

"Thank you, Dr. Phelan! **You are a lifesaver!**"

What experts are saying:

"**This book is easy to read and navigate**. As an in-home therapist I need lots of parent-friendly tools to use with families, and this is one of them. **I highly recommend it!**"

"As a parent and a school social worker, I highly recommend this book/system to everyone."

"**A wonderful book to use with parents in therapy** to assist with parenting skills."

"As a school guidance counselor, **I highly recommend this book** to both parents and teachers."

"Great book! **I am a pediatrician and I recommend it to my patients.**"

"**I've recommended this book for years** in my practice as a psychotherapist."

"**This is a staple** in my child therapy practice's pantry of goods."

"As a pediatrician, **I believe all caretakers should read *1-2-3 Magic*** and I cannot recommend it highly enough."

"As a mental health professional, I've found *1-2-3 Magic* to be **the most powerful method** of managing kids aged 2-12 that I've ever come across."

1-2-3 MAGIC

The New **3-Step Discipline**
for Calm, Effective,
and Happy Parenting

Revised 6th Edition

THOMAS W. PHELAN, PhD

Copyright © 2016 by ParentMagic, Inc.
Cover and internal design © 2016 by Sourcebooks
Cover design by Heather Morris/Sourcebooks

Sourcebooks and the colophon are registered trademarks of Sourcebooks.

All rights reserved. No part of this book may be reproduced in any form or by any electronic or mechanical means including information storage and retrieval systems—except in the case of brief quotations embodied in critical articles or reviews—without permission in writing from its publisher, Sourcebooks.

This publication is designed to provide accurate and authoritative information in regard to the subject matter covered. It is sold with the understanding that the publisher is not engaged in rendering legal, accounting, or other professional service. If legal advice or other expert assistance is required, the services of a competent professional person should be sought. —*From a Declaration of Principles Jointly Adopted by a Committee of the American Bar Association and a Committee of Publishers and Associations*

Any resemblance between persons described in this book and actual persons, living or dead, is unintentional. This book is not intended to replace appropriate diagnosis and/or treatment by a qualified mental health professional or physician.

All brand names and product names used in this book are trademarks, registered trademarks, or trade names of their respective holders. Sourcebooks is not associated with any product or vendor in this book.

Published by Sourcebooks
P.O. Box 4410, Naperville, Illinois 60567-4410
(630) 961-3900
sourcebooks.com

Library of Congress Cataloging-in-Publication Data

Phelan, Thomas W., author.
 1-2-3 magic : 3-step discipline for calm, effective, and happy parenting / Thomas W. Phelan, PhD. -- Sixth edition.
       pages cm
 Includes bibliographical references and index.
 (trade paper : alk. paper) -- (hardcover : alk. paper) 1. Discipline of children. 2. Child rearing. 3. Parenting. I. Title.
 HQ770.4.P485 2016
 649'.1--dc23

2015021612

Printed and bound in the United States of America.
WOZ 27

To Eileen

CONTENTS

Preface — xi
Introduction: Parenting: Long Hours, No Pay, Excellent Benefits — xix

Part I: Building a Solid Foundation for Parenting — 1
Chapter 1: Orientation to the Parenting Profession — 3
Chapter 2: Your Job as a Parent — 8
Chapter 3: Challenging the Little Adult Assumption — 15
Chapter 4: Avoiding the Two Biggest Discipline Mistakes — 21

Part II: Controlling Obnoxious Behavior: Parenting Job 1 — 25
Chapter 5: Getting Results through Counting — 27
Chapter 6: Advice for Nearly Any Counting Challenge — 43
Chapter 7: Disciplining Your Child in Public — 66
    Real-Life Story 1: The Case of the Temper Tantrum Terrorist — 76
Chapter 8: How to Handle Sibling Rivalry, Tantrums, Pouting, and Lying — 91
    Real-Life Story 2: The Incredible Case of the Traveling Troublemakers — 99
Chapter 9: Getting Started with Counting — 105

Part III: Managing Testing and Manipulation — 109
Chapter 10: Recognizing the Six Types of Testing and Manipulation — 111

Chapter 11: Tales from the Trenches 127

Part IV: Encouraging Good Behavior: Parenting Job 2 139
Chapter 12: Establishing Positive Routines 141
Chapter 13: Getting Up and Out in the Morning 166
Chapter 14: Cleaning Up and Chores 174
Chapter 15: Surviving Suppertime 182
Chapter 16: Tackling the Homework Problem 189
Chapter 17: Going to Bed—and Staying There! 196
    Real-Life Story 3: The Case of Bedlam at Bedtime 206
Chapter 18: Managing Your Expectations 213

Part V: Strengthening Your Relationships with Your Children: Parenting Job 3 223
Chapter 19: Sympathetic Listening 225
    Real-Life Story 4: The Case of the Fickle Friends 232
Chapter 20: The Dangers of Over-Parenting 239
Chapter 21: Real Magic: One-on-One Fun 243
Chapter 22: Solving Problems Together 248

Part VI: Enjoying Your New Family Life 255
Chapter 23: Staying Consistent 257
Chapter 24: Your Happy, Healthy Family 263

Appendix 267
Index 271
About the Author 285

PREFACE

A NUMBER OF YEARS ago a young mom came in to my office. She was a single mother of three and she was thirty-three years old. When she sat down and I had a good chance to look at her, I could see that Sarah looked like she had been run over by a truck.

When I asked the young woman what had brought her in to see me, she said, "Dr. Phelan, I don't want to get out of bed in the morning. It's horrible. I just lie there, pull the covers over my head, and cringe."

"Why don't you want to get up?" I asked.

"The thought of getting my three kids up and ready for school is horrible. It's absolutely horrible!" she said. "They don't cooperate, they fight, they treat me like I'm invisible. I scream, I yell, I nag. The whole thing is so upsetting that it ruins my day. I can't concentrate at work and I'm depressed. Then the next morning I have to do it all over again."

After asking Sarah more questions and doing a brief history of her life, I asked if she'd like to learn 1-2-3 Magic. "I'll do anything!" she said.

Sarah meant what she said. I taught her 1-2-3 Magic. She went home and told the kids things were going to be different. The kids smirked and looked at her like she was nuts.

Over the next few weeks this young mother made believers out of her three children. She used counting for sibling rivalry and disrespect. She used some of our "Start" behavior tactics for picking up, homework, and—most importantly—getting up and out in the morning. She also employed sympathetic listening and shared one-on-one fun as bonding strategies.

Sarah was a trouper. As she revolutionized her home life, we started spacing out our sessions since she didn't need to come in as often.

One day early in January, Sarah came in for her last visit. She no longer looked like she'd been run over by a truck. As she sat down, I asked her how things were going.

"Really well," she said.

"Well, that's saying something," I pointed out, "especially since you just spent two weeks with your kids over Christmas vacation."

"Yep, it went well," she said. "I've come a long way."

Then she hesitated. "But you know something?" she added. "I didn't realize how far I'd come until after they went back to school after Christmas vacation."

"What do you mean?" I asked.

A little teary, she paused, then said, "I missed them for the first time in my life."

What Can 1-2-3 Magic Do for You?

If you are raising young children, the 1-2-3 Magic program might be your ticket to effective and enjoyable parenting for several reasons:

1. The book has sold more than *1.6 million* copies.
2. *1-2-3 Magic* has been translated into *twenty-two languages*.
3. Over the last several years, *1-2-3 Magic* has consistently been the *number one child discipline book* on Amazon.com.
4. The program is *dad-friendly*.
5. It's evidence-based—that means *it works*.

For Best Results

This edition of *1-2-3 Magic* describes straightforward methods for managing the behavior of children from the ages of approximately two to twelve, whether they're average or special-needs kids. You can actually start at about eighteen months with a typically developing child. To get the best results, keep in mind the following:

1. The strategies should be used exactly as they are described here, especially with regard to the No Talking and No Emotion Rules.
2. If both parents are living at home, ideally both adults should use the program. If one parent refuses to use 1-2-3 Magic, however, the other parent can still use it on his or her own (while hoping, of course, that the partner or spouse is doing something reasonable with the kids).
3. Single, separated, and divorced parents can use our methods effectively by themselves. It is preferable if all parents—even if they are in different locations—are using the same program, but that isn't always possible. In fact, single parents greatly benefit from a simple and effective system like 1-2-3 Magic. If you are parenting on your own, you are very likely to feel overloaded, and you don't have a lot of time to spend learning discipline programs. Also, because you're by yourself, you cannot afford to be inefficient in managing your children. You only have so much energy!
4. Grandparents, babysitters, and other caregivers have also found the 1-2-3 program very helpful in managing young children. Actually, many grandparents first discovered 1-2-3 Magic on their own and then shared it with their children. In addition, we hear more and more these days that grandparents are raising their grandchildren themselves, and these adults often find 1-2-3 Magic to be a lifesaver.
5. Make sure your kids are in good physical health. It is a well-known fact that illness, allergies, and physical pain can aggravate

both behavioral and emotional problems in children. Regular physical exams for the kids are of critical importance. It's also important to know and respect your children's natural daily rhythms regarding food, sleep, and bathroom. A child who missed a nap, who feels hungry, or who has to go to the bathroom can be much more challenging to parent.

Time-Out vs. BreakTime

The revised sixth edition of *1-2-3 Magic* abandons the traditional view of time-out, which during the last fifteen to twenty years or so has become an outdated and distorted straw man that is no longer functional but all too easy to disparage. In the popular consciousness, time-out has come to be perceived as involving the following:

1. Administration by an angry, fed-up, and self-righteous parent.
2. Painful and harmful isolation of the child from the family (shunning).
3. No explanation given.
4. Harsh punishment with consequences similar to emotional child abuse.
5. Child is expected to spend time-out thinking over his misbehavior.
6. After time-out, child discusses positive behavior plans for the future with parent or other caregiver.
7. Time-out always used as first resort.
8. Parent's message: "I don't like you or your behavior."
9. Behavior dictates time-out, with no opportunity to correct.

We will replace this antiquated time-out notion with a new concept called BreakTime (or rest period). Our BreakTime idea has the following characteristics:

1. Administration by a friendly but firm parent who understands two things: (a) kids will be kids and (b) kids need limits.

2. Temporary and brief separation of the people in conflict so both can self-calm and regroup.
3. Explanation given if necessary.
4. Temporary suspension of fun activities—all is forgiven/forgotten after.
5. Child is not expected to plan behavioral reform during rest period.
6. After break, misbehavior is not discussed unless it was new, unusual, or dangerous.
7. BreakTime can be used after ignoring, distraction, sympathetic listening, joint problem solving, or two counts have been tried. If tactics other than counting routinely and rapidly produce the Talk-Persuade-Argue-Yell-Hit! Syndrome, counting and BreakTime should be moved up on the intervention list.
8. Parent's message: "I love you, but your behavior is unacceptable."
9. Only major misbehavior dictates immediate break; minor misbehaviors receive two warnings (counts) before child is vulnerable to consequence.

A parent using the traditional and distorted time-out method unrealistically and angrily expects that this intervention—often with an accompanying lecture—will end this misbehavior now, and if it doesn't, there will be hell to pay next time. A parent using BreakTime, on the other hand, knows that gentle repetition is required for kids' behavior to mature.

1-2-3 Magic and Your Child's Growing Brain

We all have a brain. One of the coolest things about our brains is the way they are unique and moldable. Your child's brain is growing and developing rapidly. It can change based on feedback from the environment. Sometimes that feedback comes from taste, touch, or smell, and sometimes it comes from the responses of people. As a parent, you are in a unique position to teach your child's brain how to grow.

1-2-3 Magic will help you gently guide your child's developing brain as it learns to manage thoughts, emotions, and behavior.

The brain has many parts that connect via pathways. No one part works in isolation. Instead, the parts talk to one another to produce behaviors, thoughts, and emotions. The brain has four lobes and two hemispheres, or sides. It has parts for movement, sensation, emotion, learning and memory, routines, body regulation, and organizing and controlling the rest of the brain.

The part of the brain that organizes and controls all this is the frontal lobe. Because it is responsible for controlling all these things, the frontal lobe can get backed up. The brain has difficulty handling emotion at the same time it controls behavior or thinking. That's why you have trouble reasoning when you're really angry and why your child can't behave rationally when they get upset.

The parts of our brains "talk" to one another using cells called neurons. There are billions and billions of neurons, and they use electrical and chemical messages to communicate across pathways. Many of them talk at the same time, and things can get dicey!

That's why there's *1-2-3 Magic*. As kids grow, the idea is for their brains to learn to organize and control the "talking" of all these neurons. With *1-2-3 Magic*, you help kids' brains mature by *anticipating* what's going to happen (like bedtime), *categorizing* new information (does it feel good or bad?), *expressing emotion* (like anxiety or joy), and *holding back* responses (like whining!) when necessary.

When you use 1-2-3 strategies such as praise, sympathetic listening, BreakTime, natural consequences, or charting, you're helping your child identify what to do and what not to do. This changes how their brain connects! As you use the behavior management techniques described in this book and bond more and more with your children, you're teaching your child's brain how to self-control, self-start, and get along with others.

1-2-3 Magic will actually help you shape the neurons in your child's brain into the right pathways. Positive behavior becomes easier and easier for the kids and you enjoy each other—a lot.

A Note about Psychological Evaluation and Counseling

Some parents may wonder: When in the process of using 1-2-3 Magic is it necessary to get a mental health professional involved?

Psychological evaluation and counseling are recommended *before* using 1-2-3 Magic if any child has a history of excessive separation anxiety, physical violence, or extremely self-punitive behavior. These children can be very difficult to manage during the initial testing period when they are still adjusting to the new discipline.

If your family is *currently* in counseling, this program should be discussed with the counselor before you use it. If your counselor is not familiar with 1-2-3 Magic, take a copy of this book, the DVD, or the audio CD for him or her to become familiar with.

Psychological evaluation and counseling are recommended *after* using 1-2-3 Magic if:

1. Marital instability or conflict is interfering with the effective use of the methods. 1-2-3 Magic is normally an excellent way to get Mom and Dad on the same page in dealing with the kids. Sometimes just a few counseling sessions can help right the ship.
2. One or both parents are incapable of following the No Talking and No Emotion Rules. (See chapter 4.) Life stressors, as well as problems such as anxiety and depression, can make it hard for some parents to calm down enough to effectively use 1-2-3 Magic. Drug and alcohol use can also make moms and dads volatile, obnoxious, and ineffective.
3. Behavior problems, as well as testing and manipulation by the child, are continuing at too high a level for more than three weeks after starting the program. Your child was hard to manage before 1-2-3 Magic. Now he's better, but you still feel managing him is too much of a grind. Check it out with a professional.
4. Trust your instincts. Here's a good rule of thumb: if you have been worrying about a particular problem in your child *for more*

than six months, that's too long. See a mental health professional and find out if there is, in fact, something wrong. If there is, try to fix it or learn how to manage it. If there's nothing wrong, stop worrying.

Serious psychological and behavioral problems in young children frequently include persistent difficulties with the following:

- Paying attention or sitting still
- Language development, social interaction, and restricted interests
- Negative, hostile, and defiant behavior
- Excessive worrying or unusual anxiety about separation
- Loss of interest in fun activities and irritability
- Excessive verbal and physical aggression
- Disregard for age-appropriate norms and rules
- Unexpected learning difficulties

INTRODUCTION

Parenting: Long Hours, No Pay, Excellent Benefits

IF YOU ASK ANY parent in this country today if they want to enjoy their children, they will look at you like you're crazy. "Enjoy my own kids? Of course I want to enjoy them. I love my kids. They're only going to be living with me for a short time."

These comments reflect parents' appreciation of their children as precious, small creatures who can be incredibly cute and adorable. But if you've been a parent for any length of time at all, you know that these priceless little beings can also be incredibly difficult. They can whine, tantrum, and tease their siblings; they can refuse to eat, do their homework, pick up, or stay in bed. At these times you still love your children, but they are definitely not enjoyable to be with.

Over the past forty years, my goal has been to help parents enjoy their kids by teaching frustrated adults simple, gentle, and evidence-based methods for managing children's difficult behavior. I have lived to see my goal fulfilled. *1-2-3 Magic* has sold two million copies, and the program has been translated into more than twenty-two foreign languages.

I love to hear comments from parents who tell me that *1-2-3*

Magic allowed them to take delight in their kids again. At professional trade shows for pediatricians, child psychiatrists, clinical psychologists, school psychologists, licensed counselors, and social workers, for example, and in communications via regular mail, email, and sites like Facebook, I have heard hundreds of times comments like these: "*1-2-3 Magic* saved my marriage!" "Super simple but really does work." "Best parenting book I have read!" and "Thanks for giving me back my four-year-old!"

Receiving feedback like that has been a deep, heartwarming, and fun experience.

The 1-2-3 Magic parenting concept really took off in the 1990s, and it continues to resonate today. Sure, parenting has become complicated by our faster-paced digital world, but moms and dads are still faced with the same basic issues parents have always had to deal with. Two thousand years ago, parents in the Roman Empire had to find ways to get their kids to sleep through the night. Medieval parents had to deal with pouting, yelling, and ferocious sibling rivalry. Italian moms and dads during the Renaissance were driven crazy by whining and tantrums, and kids during the French Revolution argued, whined, refused to eat their vegetables, and continually messed up their *maisons* (houses).

Today, the remarkable effectiveness of *1-2-3 Magic* continues to rest upon this bedrock: this is the only parenting program based on the fact that parents talk too much. Automatic parental chatter, prattle, babble, or whatever you want to call it is too often parents' disciplinary default in these modern times, and this approach too often leads to ineffectiveness and even disaster (spanking, child abuse). Those outcomes are definitely not enjoyable.

This new edition of *1-2-3 Magic* represents the best of my forty years of child discipline experience as a parent, clinical psychologist, author, speaker, and social media maniac. In this new edition, you'll also become familiar with the "brain-based" part of the 1-2-3 Magic program. We tried to keep our answer to this question as simple as possible, but exactly how does 1-2-3 Magic interact with a child's developing brain in ways that produce cooperation, independence, social skills, and emotional intelligence? You'll be surprised to learn how it works!

So, how do you enjoy your precious little ones during the short time they live in your house? You learn specific tactics and routines for handling your three fundamental parenting jobs: managing obnoxious behavior (arguing, yelling, whining, fighting, pouting), encouraging positive behavior (getting up and out, eating, doing homework, picking up, going to bed—and staying there!), and parent/child bonding. It takes about five hours to learn via book, audiobook, DVD, or streaming video—formats we have created to make sure all parents can learn the program through whichever media they prefer.

Kids are cute. They can also be tons of fun—if you know what you're doing!

PART I

Building a Solid Foundation for Parenting

CHAPTER 1
Orientation to the Parenting Profession

CHAPTER 2
Your Job as a Parent

CHAPTER 3
Challenging the Little Adult Assumption

CHAPTER 4
Avoiding the Two Biggest Discipline Mistakes

1
ORIENTATION TO THE PARENTING PROFESSION

How to Prepare for the World's Most Important Job

THERE'S NO WAY TO know what parenting is like until you do it. Whatever thoughts you may have had about becoming a mom or a dad, bringing that first child home is a jolt—a big jolt. The only guarantee is that raising your child will be more difficult, and more rewarding, than you could ever have expected.

1-2-3 Magic is based on the idea that parenting should be looked at as a profession. In other words, some training will make the job much easier. But that training shouldn't have to take years or involve bringing tons of books home from the library. One book should do it.

Ground Rules for Effective Parenting

The place to start is with your basic parenting philosophy—your overall orientation to the job, which provides the ground rules. Even though the job changes as the kids get older, effective parents have two important qualities. They are:

1. **Warm and friendly on the one hand.**
2. **Demanding and firm on the other.**

Being *warm and friendly* means taking care of kids' emotional and physical needs. It means feeding them, keeping them safe, warm, and well clothed, and making sure they get enough sleep. Warmth and friendliness also mean being sensitive to the children's feelings: sharing their joy over a new friend, comforting them when their ice cream falls on the ground, listening sympathetically when they're angry at their teacher, and enjoying their company.

Being warm and friendly also means *liking*—not just loving—your children.

The other important parental trait, being *demanding and firm*, is meant in the good sense. Good parents expect something from their kids. They expect good behavior in school, respect toward adults, hard work on academics, effort in sports, and relationships with friends that include sharing and kindness. They expect their children to follow the rules, to do things for other people, and to sometimes confront issues that are hard or scary.

In other words, effective parents expect their children to rise to life's challenges (as you know, there are plenty!) and to respect the rules and limits that will be required for their behavior.

These two parental orientations, warm-friendly and demanding-firm, might at first seem contradictory. They are not. Some situations call for one, some for the other, and some situations require both. For example, what if your daughter, Megan, slaps her brother, Jon? Time for the demanding side of parenting. But if Megan feeds the dog without being asked? Time for the warm side.

What if it's time for bed? Both friendly and firm sides are necessary. The friendly side might mean snuggling in bed with a child for fifteen minutes of story time before lights-out. The demanding side, on the other hand, might mean requiring the kids to get ready for bed (teeth, bath or shower, pajamas, and so on) *before* story time can happen. And at nine o'clock, firm means lights-out. No ifs, ands, or buts.

The messages this parenting philosophy sends to children are:

1. **Warm-friendly: I love you and I'll take care of you.**
2. **Demanding-firm: I expect something from you.**

Why are both the warm-friendly and demanding-firm attitudes toward your children necessary? For two reasons. The first reason is simple: fun! It would be nice if you could enjoy the children while they are growing up in your household. Kids are energetic, cute, exciting, and fun, and you can have great times with them you'll never forget.

The second reason is a bit sad. You want your children to grow up, leave home someday, and make it on their own. Warm and demanding, therefore, also means *encouraging and respecting your kids' growing independence*. Friendly and firm means not hovering and not being overprotective. It means giving children a chance to do things more and more on their own as they get older. When our oldest walked five blocks to kindergarten on the first day of school, I was sure he was never coming back. He came back just fine, and I learned a lesson about independence and about his growing competence.

> **Key Concept**
> Research has shown that effective parents are warm and friendly on the one hand, but also demanding and firm on the other. Both orientations are critical to raising emotionally intelligent and mature kids.

Automatic vs. Deliberate Parenting

You might say there are two kinds of parenting modes: automatic and deliberate. Automatic parenting includes the things you do spontaneously without really thinking (and with no real training), such as picking up and comforting a sobbing two-year-old who has just fallen down. Comforting an upset child is a positive example, but automatic parenting can also include actions that aren't so useful, such as screaming at a seven-year-old who keeps getting out of bed because she says she hears a noise in her closet.

Here's what you'll want to do with the 1-2-3 Magic program:

1. Hang on to your positive automatic parenting habits. You'll find that some of your beneficial parenting moves are already part of the program, such as being a good listener or praising your kids' efforts.
2. Identify your automatic parenting habits that are harmful, useless, or upsetting. As you read through this book, decide how you'll replace these negative actions with deliberate, respectful, and more useful 1-2-3 Magic strategies.
3. Practice, practice, practice! Work hard and thoughtfully until the new methods become automatic. Because 1-2-3 Magic works so well, it tends to be self-reinforcing, which makes the deliberate-to-automatic conversion much easier.

> **Quik Tip**
> Identify your automatic parenting habits that are harmful, useless, or upsetting. As you read *1-2-3 Magic*, decide how you'll replace these negative actions with deliberate, respectful, and more useful strategies.

Automatic parenting includes another critically important activity that you do all the time: *modeling*. Children are great imitators, and they learn a lot by just watching the way you behave. If you are respectful toward others, your kids will tend to be the same. If you scream in fury during fits of road rage, on the other hand... Well, you get the idea.

The goal, therefore, is effective, automatic parenting. This approach takes some concentration and effort in the beginning, but in the end it's a whole lot less work. And you and your family are a whole lot better off!

Your Child's Developing Brain

Your child's brain is growing and developing rapidly, and it uses up tons of energy! As a parent, you are in a unique position to teach your child's brain how to grow by enabling it to control thoughts, feelings, and behavior. Two of the most important ways in which you do this are by modeling these critical skills and by using the warm and demanding parenting model when you are dealing with your kids.

The "CEO" of your brain and of your child's brain is called the frontal cortex. The frontal cortex is the organizer of all kinds of sensory, emotional, thought, and behavioral information. The different parts of any human brain "talk" to one another by using specialized cells called neurons that communicate across pathways using both chemical and electrical messages. *1-2-3 Magic* will help your child's brain organize its experience in ways that promote positive behavior, emotional control, and good relationships with other people.

CHAPTER SUMMARY

2

YOUR JOB AS A PARENT

Three Things You Can Do to Raise Happy, Healthy Kids

WE HAVE THREE SEPARATE parenting jobs that require different strategies. Each of these parenting jobs is distinct, manageable, and important. They also are interdependent; each relies to some extent on the others for its success. Ignore any of these tasks at your own risk! Do these three well, and you'll be a pretty good mom or dad. The first two parenting jobs involve discipline and behavior concerns, while the third focuses on the parent-child relationship.

- **Parenting Job 1** involves *controlling obnoxious behavior*. You will never like or get along well with your children if they are constantly irritating you with behavior such as whining, arguing, teasing, badgering, tantrums, yelling, and fighting. In this book you will learn how to use the 1-2-3 counting technique to control obnoxious behavior, and you will be pleasantly surprised at how effective that simple technique is!
- **Parenting Job 2** involves *encouraging good behavior*. Encouraging good behavior—such as picking up toys, going to bed, being

courteous, and doing homework—requires more effort by parents (and more effort from kids to engage in the encouraged behavior) than controlling difficult behavior does. In this book, you will learn seven simple methods for encouraging positive actions in your kids.

- **Parenting Job 3** is *strengthening your relationship with your children*. Some parents merely need to be reminded of Parenting Job 3; other parents have to work hard at remembering to do it. Paying attention to the quality of your relationship with your children will help you with Jobs 1 and 2, and vice versa.

How do our three parenting jobs relate to the warm and demanding parenting traits? As you may have guessed already, the tactic for Job 1, controlling obnoxious behavior, depends almost entirely on the demanding parent role. There's not much warm or fuzzy about it! Job 3, however, will rely almost entirely on the warm side of the parenting equation. And finally, Job 2, encouraging good behavior, will employ both warm and demanding strategies.

> **Quik Tip**
> Some parents only need a simple reminder about Parenting Job 3: strengthening your relationship with your children. However, other parents have to work hard at remembering to do it.

Stop vs. Start Behavior

When it comes to discipline, children present two basic problems to adults, and these two problems define the first two parenting tasks. When we are frustrated with our children, the kids are either (1) doing something negative we want them to *Stop* (like whining), or (2) *not* doing something positive we would like them to *Start* (like getting dressed). In 1-2-3 Magic, we call these two kinds of things "Stop" behavior and "Start" behavior. In the hustle and bustle of everyday existence, you may not have worried much about the difference between Start and Stop behaviors, but—as we'll soon see—the distinction is extremely important.

Parenting Job 1: Controlling Obnoxious Behavior

Parenting Job 1, and the first step in getting your family back on track, is controlling your children's obnoxious behavior, or Stop behavior. Stop behavior includes frequent, minor, everyday issues, such as whining, disrespect, tantrums, arguing, teasing, fighting, pouting, yelling, and so on. Stop behavior—in and of itself—ranges from mildly irritating to pretty obnoxious. Each of these difficult behaviors may not be so bad on its own, but add them all up in one afternoon and by 5:00 p.m. you may feel like hitchhiking to South America.

For Stop behavior, such as whining, arguing, screaming, and teasing, use the 1-2-3, or "counting" procedure. Counting is simple, gentle, and direct.

Strategies for Controlling Obnoxious Behavior

For **Stop** behavior, such as:
Whining
Teasing
Arguing
Pouting
Yelling
Tantrums

Use the 1-2-3 or "counting" procedure.

Parenting Job 2: Encouraging Positive Behavior

The second parenting job is to encourage your children's positive behavior, or Start behavior. Start behavior includes positive activities like cleaning rooms, doing homework, practicing the piano, getting up and out in the morning, going to bed, eating supper, and being nice to other people. You have a Start behavior problem when your child is not doing something that would be a good thing to do.

For Start behavior problems, you will have a choice of seven tactics, which can be used either one at a time or in combination. These tactics are **praise, simple requests, kitchen timers, the docking system, natural consequences, charting,** and **the counting variation**. Start behavior strategies, as you can probably guess, require a little more thought and effort than counting does.

Strategies for Encouraging Good Behavior

For **Start** behavior, such as:
Picking up
Eating
Homework
Bedtime
Up and out in the morning

Use praise, simple requests, kitchen timers, the docking system, natural consequences, charting, and the counting variation.

Choosing Your Strategy

Why the difference in strategies between Parenting Jobs 1 and 2? The answer lies in the issue of motivation. If she is motivated, how long does it take a child to terminate an irritating Stop behavior like whining, arguing, or teasing? The answer is about one second.

It's really not a big project. Depending on how angry or oppositional a child is, ending an occurrence of obnoxious behavior doesn't take tons of effort.

But now look at Start behavior. How long does it take a child to accomplish something constructive, like eating dinner? Maybe twenty to twenty-five minutes. To pick up after himself? Perhaps fifteen minutes. To get ready for bed? Twenty to thirty minutes. Ready for school? Thirty minutes. Homework? Schoolwork might take anywhere from forty minutes to three years. So it's obvious that with Start behavior, more motivation is required from the child. He has to begin the project, keep at it, and then finish. And the project is often something the child is not thrilled about having to do in the first place.

In addition, if encouraging positive behavior in kids requires more motivation from the kids, it's also going to require more motivation from Mom and Dad. As you'll soon see, putting an end to Stop behavior by counting is relatively easy if you do it right. Start behavior requires more sophisticated tactics.

In managing a behavioral difficulty with one of your children, you will need to first determine if you have a Stop or a Start behavior problem. "Is the issue something I want the child to quit? Or is it something I want him or her to get going on?" Since counting is so easy, parents sometimes make the mistake of using counting for Start behavior (for example, counting a child to get her to do her homework).

As you will soon see, counting produces motivation that usually lasts only a short time (from a few seconds to a couple of minutes) in children and does not provide the lasting motivation needed to get a child to continue desired behavior. If you mix up your tactics (such as using the counting technique for homework), you will not get optimum results.

But don't worry. This whole procedure is so simple that you'll be an expert in no time. Effective discipline will start to come naturally and—believe it or not—your kids will start listening to you.

Parenting Job 3: Strengthening Your Relationships

Your final parenting job is to work on strengthening your relationship with your kids. This means making sure that screen time does not replace face-to-face time. More importantly, strengthening relationships means that you value enjoying one another's company. It is critical to your family's well-being and to your kids' self-esteem that you like (not just love) your children.

What does "liking" your children mean? Here's an example. It's a Saturday and you're home by yourself for a few hours—a rare occurrence! Everyone has gone out. You're listening to some music and just puttering around. You hear a noise outside and look out to see a car pulling up in the driveway. One of your kids gets out and heads for the front door.

How do you feel in your gut right at that moment? If it's "Oh no, the fun's over!" that may not be *like*. If it's "Oh good, I've got some company!" that's more like *like*.

Liking your children and having a good relationship with them is important for lots of reasons. The most important reason may be that it's simply more fun. Kids are naturally cute and enjoyable a lot of the time, and you want to take advantage of that valuable quality. And they only grow up with you once.

Strategies for Strengthening Your Relationships:

Practice sympathetic listening
Avoid over-parenting
Join in one-on-one fun
Solve problems together

1-2-3 Magic Will Change Your Child's Brain—and Your Brain!

It may surprise you to learn that this program will also help *your* brain and your child's brain. Your three parenting jobs will take up a lot of mental energy—both for your kids and for you. Job #1, for example, shows you how to teach your child's brain and your own brain how to hold back and control certain kinds of dysfunctional responses. Research shows that stopping behaviors is hard—it requires a lot of brainpower from the CEO, the frontal cortex. Not yelling, for instance, is hard for moms and dads!

Job #2 trains children and parents about what to do regarding positive behavior. Parental strategies such as praise, warmth, and structure actually help provide extra power to your child's brain to help it carry out Start behaviors, which often require sustained effort.

Emotional stability provides a secure base so your child's brain can learn and grow and so you can enjoy your kids. Parenting Job #3, bonding with your children, goes a long way toward making that kind of environment available.

Next up? In chapter 3 we'll examine the strange and amazingly disruptive idea that adults carry around in their brains about small children.

CHAPTER SUMMARY

Have you ever felt overwhelmed by the importance and magnitude of the job of parenting? From now on, just focus on managing difficult behavior, promoting positive behavior, and strengthening relationships. That focus will make the task feel much more manageable. The rest of the time? Just be yourself!

3
CHALLENGING THE LITTLE ADULT ASSUMPTION

Why You Need to Remember
That Kids Are Just Kids

THERE IS AN ENCHANTING but troublesome idea that parents and teachers carry around in their heads about young children. This naive assumption—or wish—causes not only discipline failures, but also stormy scenes that can include physical child abuse. The idea we're talking about is known as the "Little Adult Assumption."

The Little Adult Assumption is the belief that kids are basically reasonable and unselfish. In other words, they're just smaller versions of grown-ups. And because they are little adults, the reasoning goes, whenever children misbehave, the problem must be that they don't have enough information in their heads to be able to do the right thing. The solution? Simply give them the facts.

Imagine, for example, that at exactly 4:12 p.m. your eight-year-old son is teasing his five-year-old sister for the eighteenth time since they got home from school. What should you do? If your boy is a little adult, you simply sit him down, calmly look him in the eye, and explain to him the three golden reasons why he shouldn't tease his sister. First of all, teasing hurts her. Second, it makes you mad at him. Third—and most important—how would he feel if someone treated him like that?

Now imagine further that after this explanation your son looks at you—his face brightening with insight—and he says, "Gee, I never looked at it like that before!" Then he stops bothering his sibling for the rest of his life. That would certainly be nice, but any veteran parent or teacher knows that doesn't happen. Kids are not little adults.

The crucial point here is this: grown-ups who want to believe the Little Adult Assumption are going to rely heavily on *words and reasons* in dealing with young kids. And by themselves, words and reasons are going to be miserable failures much of the time. Sometimes explanations will have absolutely no impact at all. At other times adult attempts at enlightenment will take parent and child through what we call the "Talk-Persuade-Argue-Yell-Hit Syndrome."

> **Quik Tip**
> Adults who believe in the Little Adult Assumption are going to rely heavily on words and reasons in trying to change the behavior of young kids. And words and reasons are going to be miserable failures much of the time.

Imagine this: your child is doing something you don't like. A parenting book said you should talk the problem out no matter how long it takes. So you try telling your five-year-old daughter why she shouldn't be disrespectful. She doesn't respond, so you next try to persuade her to see things your way. When persuasion fails, you start arguing. Arguing leads to a yelling match, and when that fails, you may feel there is nothing left to do but hit her to get the results you want.

Actually, the vast majority of the time when parents scream, hit, and spank their children, the parent is simply having a temper tantrum. The tantrum is a sign that (1) the parent doesn't know what to do, (2) the parent is so frustrated that he or she can't see straight, and (3) this adult may have an anger-management problem.

We're not implying that you go around hitting your kids all the time. However, the chief cause of child abuse (physical abuse, not sexual) may be the Little Adult Assumption. A parent reads in a book that reasoning is the preferred method. When reasoning fails, the parent resorts to physical violence, because his favorite strategy isn't working and desperation has set in.

The acts of talking and explaining certainly have their place in raising children. But kids are just kids—not little adults. Years ago one writer said, "Childhood is a period of transitory psychosis." She meant that when they are little, kids are—in a way—basically nuts! They are not born reasonable and unselfish; they are born unreasonable and selfish. They want what they want when they want it, and they will have a major fit if they don't get it. Consequently, it is the parent's job—and the teacher's job—to help kids gradually learn frustration tolerance. In accomplishing this goal, adults need to be gentle, consistent, decisive, and calm.

How do you do that? You start by changing your thinking about children and by getting rid of the Little Adult Assumption. To get this crazy and harmful notion out of parents' heads, we use a bit of what we call "cognitive shock therapy." Although it may sound strange, think of it like this: instead of imagining your kids as little adults, think of yourself as a *wild animal trainer*! Of course, we don't mean using whips, guns, or chairs. And we certainly don't mean being nasty.

> **Caution**
> One explanation, if really necessary, is fine. It's the attempts at *repeated explanations* that get adults and kids into trouble. Too much parent talking irritates and distracts children.

But what does a wild animal trainer do? He chooses a method—which is largely nonverbal—and repeats it until the "trainee" does what the trainer wants. The trainer is patient, gentle, and persistent. Our job in this book is to present some training methods to you, so that you can repeat them until the trainees (your children) do what you want them to.

Fortunately, you do not usually have to repeat these methods for very long before you get results. And you can gradually add more talking and reasoning into your strategy as the kids get older. But remember this: one explanation—if necessary—is fine. It's the attempts at repeated explanations that get adults and children in trouble.

From Dictatorship to Democracy

The overall orientation of 1-2-3 Magic is what you might call "dictatorship to democracy." When your kids are little, your house should be pretty much a benign dictatorship where you are the judge and jury. Your four-year-old, for example, cannot unilaterally choose—at seven thirty in the morning on Wednesday—to skip preschool because she wants to stay home and play with her new birthday stuff.

When the kids are in their mid to late teens, however, your house should be more of a democracy. Teenagers should have more say about the rules that affect them. You should have family meetings to iron out differences. Even when the kids are teens, though, when push comes to shove, who's paying the mortgage? You are. And who knows better than the kids what's good for them? You do. When necessary, you have a right—and a duty—to impose limits on your children, even if they don't like it.

> **Key Concept**
> Noncompliance and lack of cooperation in children are not always due to lack of information. Kids are not little adults or simply small computers, so raising children involves training as well as explaining.

Too many parents these days are afraid of their children. What are they afraid of? Physical attack? Not usually. What many parents fear is that their children won't like them. So, in a conflict situation, these parents explain and explain and explain, hoping the child will eventually come around and say something like, "Gee, I never looked at it like that before." All too often, these parental efforts simply lead to the Talk-Persuade-Argue-Yell-Hit Syndrome.

What if you have children who always respond to words and

reasons? You are certainly lucky! Recent research has indicated that there are exactly three such children in the country. If you have one or more of them, you may not need this book. Or, if your kids stop responding to logic, you can consider using the 1-2-3 program.

So what is the training method we're talking about? We first have to explain what it is not.

Your Chatter Can Overwhelm Your Child's Brain

Kids' ability to use abstract language is not fully formed until a child is around age twelve, and this maturing process can go on until your child becomes a young adult in their early twenties. This means that in an emotional situation, when you provide lengthy and complicated explanations as a disciplinary device, you are overloading your child's young brain. In other words, rather than helping the situation, you are making it worse.

Your child's frontal cortex is not capable of processing a lot of words while trying to calm down and manage emotion at the same time. Even though the actual words a parent uses may be perfectly logical, the overload results in an angrier, overwhelmed child and an even more frustrated mom or dad.

CHAPTER SUMMARY
What's wrong with this picture?

4
AVOIDING THE TWO BIGGEST DISCIPLINE MISTAKES

The Dangers of Too Much Talking and Too Much Emotion

THE TWO BIGGEST DISCIPLINE mistakes that parents and other caretakers make in dealing with young children are (1) too much talking and (2) too much emotion. Thinking of kids as little adults and then chattering away during a situation requiring discipline is bad because excessive explaining makes kids *less likely to cooperate* by irritating, confusing, and distracting them. Endless chatter also leads to the Talk-Persuade-Argue-Yell-Hit Syndrome.

But why is too much adult emotion bad during discipline? People today tell you to "let it all hang out" and show your feelings. "Express yourself and don't keep it all inside" seems to be the universal recommendation of modern psychology.

Is this a good suggestion if you are a parent? One half of it is good advice and the other half is not. The good half is this: if you are feeling positively toward a child, by all means let it show. Express your affection or dole out some praise. The bad half of the let-it-all-hang-out advice applies to times when you are irritated or angry with your children. Cutting loose at these moments can be a problem, because when we parents are mad we often do the wrong thing. Angry adults can yell, scream, belittle, and nag. They can also physically endanger their kids. The 1-2-3 program is as much a control on parental anger as it is a control on children's behavior.

Why Your Kids Like to Upset You

There is another reason why too much emotion can interfere with effective parenting and effective teaching. When they are little, kids feel inferior to adults. They feel inferior because they *are* inferior. They are smaller, less privileged, less intelligent, less skillful, less responsible, and less of just about everything than their parents and the older kids are. And this "lessness" bugs them a lot. They don't like it. They like to feel they are powerful and capable of making some mark on the world.

> **Quik Tip**
> If your little child can get big, old you all upset, your upset is the big splash for him. Your emotional outburst accidentally makes your child feel powerful.

Watch your two-year-olds. They want to be like those cool five-year-olds, who can do a lot more neat things. The five-year-olds, in turn, want to be like the cool ten-year-olds. And the ten-year-olds want to be like you. They want to drive cars and use cell phones and credit cards (and some do!). They want to have an impact on the world and to make things happen.

Have you ever seen a small child go down to a lake and throw rocks in the water? Children can do that for hours, partly because the big splashes are a sign of their impact. They are the ones causing all the commotion.

"What does this have to do with what happens at my house?" you may ask. Simple. If your little child can get big, old you all upset, *your upset is the big splash for him.* Your emotional outburst has the unintended consequence of making your child feel powerful. His reaction does not mean that he has no conscience or is going to grow up to be a professional criminal. It's just a normal childhood feeling.

Having all that power temporarily rewards—or feels good to—the inferior part of the child. Parents who say, "It drives me absolutely crazy when she eats her dinner with her fingers! Why does she do that?" may have already answered their own question. She may do that—at least partly—*because it drives Mom and Dad crazy.*

An important rule, therefore, is this: If you have a child who is doing something you don't like, get really upset about it on a regular basis and, sure enough, she'll repeat it for you.

When it comes to discipline, you want to be consistent, decisive, and calm. So what we recommend in this book is that you apply—during moments involving conflict or discipline—what we call the "No Talking and No Emotion Rules." Since we're all human, these two rules really mean very little talking and very little emotion. *But these rules are absolutely critical to your disciplinary effectiveness.* There are discipline systems other than the 1-2-3 program, but you will ruin any of them by talking too much and getting too excited. These two mistakes, of course, usually go hand in hand, and the emotion involved is usually anger.

Some parents and teachers can turn off the talking and the emotional upset like a faucet, especially once they see how effective it is to keep quiet at the right time. Other adults have to bite their lips bloody to get the job done. I saw a T-shirt a while back that said, "Help me—I'm talking and I can't stop!" Lots of moms, dads, and teachers have to remind themselves over and over and over again that talking, arguing, yelling, and screaming not only don't help, but actually make things worse. These "tactics" merely blow off steam for a few seconds. If, after a month to six weeks of using 1-2-3 Magic, parents find that they can't shake these habits, it's time to face facts. Some sort of outpatient evaluation and counseling is indicated (for the adult, not the child!).

Remember, we're talking here primarily about negative or angry emotion and talk—not positive. Good parents do express warmth and affection for their kids. They do listen sympathetically when the children are upset. Discipline and parent-child conflict situations are where you really have to watch yourself.

Kids Need Clear Signals from You

The same CEO part of your brain responsible for controlling your behavior, the frontal cortex, also controls your emotions. This applies to your brain as well as your child's brain! This mental organ can't do both things at the same time.

When you talk angrily to your child about the *reasons* for stopping an obnoxious behavior, you are irritating, confusing, and distracting your child's brain from focusing on the one thing you want the child to do—stop that behavior!

CHAPTER SUMMARY

PART II

Controlling Obnoxious Behavior

Parenting Job 1

CHAPTER 5
Getting Results through Counting

CHAPTER 6
Advice for Nearly Any Counting Challenge

CHAPTER 7
Disciplining Your Child in Public

CHAPTER 8
How to Handle Sibling Rivalry, Tantrums, Pouting, and Lying

CHAPTER 9
Getting Started with Counting

5
GETTING RESULTS THROUGH COUNTING

Sometimes Your Silence Speaks Louder Than Your Words

WHEN YOUR KIDS ARE acting up, you now know what you're not supposed to do: get excited and start chattering. But just what *are* you supposed to do?

To help with your first giant parenting job—controlling obnoxious behavior—you'll use the 1-2-3, or counting, procedure. Counting is surprisingly powerful and deceptively simple, but you have to know what you're doing for this process to be most effective. In the beginning, keep two things in mind:

- First, you will use the counting method to deal with Stop (obnoxious or difficult) behavior. In other words, you will be counting for things like arguing, fighting, whining, yelling, tantrums, and so on. You will not use the 1-2-3 method to get the child up in the morning, to get her to do her homework, or to motivate her to practice the piano.

> Second, if you are new to 1-2-3 Magic, after you learn how to do the 1-2-3 process, you will be skeptical. The procedure will seem too easy, and it may not appear aggressive or tough enough. Some of you will think, "Hey, you don't know my kid. He is a wild man!"

Don't worry about feeling skeptical. Remember, the 1-2-3 program *is* simple, but it is not always easy. The "magic" is not in the counting. Anyone can count. The magic—or what may seem like magic after you've done it for a while—is in the No Talking and No Emotion Rules. Watching you follow these rules makes children think and take responsibility for their own behavior.

Of course, there really is no magic in 1-2-3 Magic—it just seems that way. The program represents the careful, logical, and persistent extension of a special behavioral technology to the gentle discipline and training of children. Soon—when conflicts with kids arise—you will feel like a new person: consistent, decisive, and calm.

Quik Tip
Use counting only for **Stop** behavior, not for **Start** behavior.

Introduction to Counting

How does the 1-2-3 process work? Imagine you have a four-year-old child who is having a major temper tantrum on the kitchen floor at 6:00 p.m. because you—in your hardness of heart—would not let him use his favorite electronic device right before dinner. Your son is banging his head on the floor, kicking your new kitchen cabinets, and screaming bloody murder. You are sure the neighbors can hear the noise all the way down the block, and you're at a loss about what to do.

Your pediatrician told you to ignore your son's temper tantrums, but you don't think you can stand it. Your mother told you to put a cold washcloth on his face, but you think her advice is strange. And, finally, your husband told you to spank the boy.

None of these is an acceptable course of action. Instead, you hold up one finger, look down at your noisy little devil, and calmly say, "That's 1."

He doesn't care. He's insane with rage and keeps the tantrum going full blast. You let five seconds go by, then you hold up two fingers and say, "That's 2." That's all you say. But you get the same lousy reaction; the tantrum continues. So after five more seconds, you hold up three fingers and say, "That's 3. Take five."

Now what does all this mean? It means that your son was just given two chances—the first two counts—to shape up. But in this instance he blew it. He didn't stop the undesirable behavior. So there is going to be a consequence. The consequence can be a "rest period" or BreakTime (about one minute per year of the child's life), or the consequence can be what we call a "BreakTime alternative" (loss of a privilege or toy for a period of time, bedtime fifteen minutes earlier, forty cents off the allowance, no electronic entertainment for two hours, and so on.)

Let's imagine the consequence you choose is a rest period or BreakTime. After you say "That's 3. Take five," the child goes to BreakTime. (Some of you are wondering, "How do I get him there?" That question will be answered in the next chapter.)

> **Quik Tip**
> What is going to happen in a relatively short time is this: you'll start getting good control—believe it or not—at 1 or 2. And that is going to make you feel really good!

A BreakTime is a brief period where you and your child take a break from each other. A child can sit on a chair or stair, but if they won't stay put, then a play yard (like a Pack 'n Play), a bedroom, or a crib may serve the purpose better. You do not talk or make eye contact during BreakTime, but this silence is not done in an angry or punitive way. Counting and rest periods are very gentle procedures that give everyone a chance to calm down.

If you choose a child's bedroom, you do not have to close the door. With children who have a history of separation anxiety or past trauma, you would not want to close the door in the first place. You can sit quietly by the door if you wish, and if the kids don't want to stay put, there are a number of suggestions in the next chapter for managing that.

After the rest period is served, you will not believe what happens next. Nothing! No talking, no emotion, no apologies, no lectures, no discussions. Nothing is said unless the behavior is new, unusual, or dangerous.

You do not say, for example, "Now, are you going to be a good boy? Do you realize what you've been doing to your mother all afternoon? Why do we have to go through this all the time? I'm so sick and tired of this that I could scream! Your sister doesn't behave this way, and your father's coming home in half an hour. Did God put you on earth to drive me crazy or what?"

Tempting as this lecture might be, you simply keep quiet. If the child behaves, praise him and enjoy his company. If the child does something else that's countable, count it.

In a relatively short time, you'll start getting good control—believe it or not—when you count to 1 or 2. And we will promise you this: The first time you stop a fight between two of your kids from across the room, and all you have to do is say, "That's 1" or "That's 2," and you don't have to get up or yell or scream or do something worse that you'll be sorry for later... the first time you do that, you're going to feel really good!

> **Quik Tip**
> If your child does something dangerous or extreme, don't count and give them three chances to stop. Go straight to 3!

Some parents ask, "My child always takes us to 2. Don't you think he's manipulating us?" The answer is no. Why? Because what really drives people crazy is 42! Or 72—a child who has to be told a thousand times before he'll shape up. Two times is not so bad. Remember, if the child hits 3, that's it—time for a break.

Other parents ask, with good reason, "What if my son or daughter does something that's so bad I don't want to give them three chances to stop doing it?" That's a good question. For example, what if your child hits you? In that case, it would be ridiculous to say, "That's 1," and give him two more chances to sock away. If in your opinion the behavior is extraordinarily bad, you simply say, "That's 3. Take five, and add fifteen more for the seriousness of the offense."

In more recent years, some people have taken issue with the idea of what has been called time-out, saying that it is punishment and that, as such, it is harmful to kids. The fact is there is a rich literature supporting the use of time-out as a helpful and gentle way of teaching kids about good and bad behavior. The real issue here is this: there is a good way and a bad way to do time-outs, rest periods, or BreakTimes. The criticisms of the procedure are really criticisms of BreakTime done wrong.

BreakTime done wrong means the following: a consequence implemented by a parent who is furious, yelling, lecturing, or otherwise using emotionally abusive or physically abusive behavior. This kind of approach is based on shame, it teaches nothing other than how to feel bad about yourself, and it simply reflects a parent who has major anger management issues. The problem is not time-out; the problem is the major violation of our No-Talking and No-Emotion rules, which are critical to the successful use of 1-2-3 Magic. BreakTime done well is gentle, supportive, firm, and instructive.

Let's look at another example. What if your seven-year-old learns a bad word on the playground? He doesn't know what it means, but he wants to try it out on you. So at eight thirty when you say it's time to get ready for bed, he replies, "You blankity-blank!" Same thing. "That's 3. Take five, and add fifteen more for the rotten mouth." When that child returns from BreakTime, a short explanation will be in order concerning what the word meant and why he can't use it in your house. Remember: explanations are appropriate when a child's misbehavior is new, unusual, or dangerous.

That's it. That's the essence of counting. Counting is extremely simple, direct, and effective. But now you are thinking that there must be a catch. And guess what? There is.

Counting Challenges

Occasionally I have run into parents who say, "We went to your workshop about eight weeks ago, and we enjoyed it. We have two fairly difficult kids, aged seven and five. When we went home we were very surprised. 1-2-3 Magic worked, and our children were much better behaved. But that was two months ago. The 1-2-3 method is not working anymore. We need a new discipline program."

What's the problem here? Ninety percent of the time the problem is that the parents "forgot" the No Talking and No Emotion Rules. Adults can slip up like this *without even being aware of it*. Remember our four-year-old tantrum artist and the electronic device? Here's how that scene might sound if the parent is unwittingly talking too much and getting too excited while attempting to count the child's outburst:

"That's 1. Come on now, I'm getting a little tired of this. Why can't you do one little thing for us—*Look at me when I'm talking to you, young man!* OK, that's 2. One more and you're going to your room, do you hear me? I'm sick and tired of you whining and fussing over every little thing you can't have. One more and that's it. *Your sister never behaves this way... Your father's coming home in half an hour!* OK, enough! That's 3. Take five. BEAT IT! OUT OF MY SIGHT!"

What was that? That was a parental temper tantrum. Now we have two tantrums going on in the same kitchen. This adult's outburst was not the 1-2-3 program at all. What's wrong with what this angry parent just did? Three things.

If you do "communicate" like this parent just did, what you are really saying is simply this: "Let's fight!" And you don't have to have a kid with ADHD (attention deficit/hyperactivity disorder) or ODD (oppositional defiant disorder) or CD (conduct disorder)—you're still going to get a fight. Plenty of kids would rather cut off their left leg than lose a good battle of words. Unwise attempts at talking or persuading are guaranteed to take a child's focus *off* the possibility of good behavior and put it *on* the prospect of an enjoyable and energetic argument.

Second, many difficult children do have ADHD. That doesn't mean they don't *get* enough attention. It means they can't *pay* attention. Faced with that huge mass of adult words, how is an ADHD child—or any other child, for that matter—supposed to pick out the most important parts, which are the counts or warnings? He can't. Children can't respond properly to warnings if they don't hear them clearly in the first place.

Finally, even if you forget all the emotion involved, as Mom or Dad talks more and more, their basic message changes. When a parent gives lots and lots of reasons to a child regarding why he should shape up, the real message becomes: "You don't have to behave unless I can give you five or six good reasons why you should. And, gee, I certainly hope you agree with my reasons."

> **Key Concept**
> When you talk too much, you switch your child's focus off the need for good behavior and on to the possibility of an enjoyable argument.

This is not discipline. The word describing this "strategy" starts with the letter *B*. It's *begging*. When you beg like this, you are (1) trying to think for your child, (2) taking the responsibility for his behavior, and (3) really caught up in the Little Adult Assumption.

What's the average child going to do? He's going to take issue with your reasons. "Katie doesn't always do what you say. Daddy's not coming home in half an hour." Now you have, in effect, left the discipline ballpark and you're out in the street arguing. The main issue—your child's behavior—has been forgotten.

So if the child is acting up, it's "That's 1." (Bite your tongue.) Then, if necessary, "That's 2" (Easy does it; keep quiet), and so on. Count firmly but respectfully; your voice can be casual or even a little stern. Remember that the magic is not in the counting. It's in the *pregnant pause right after the warning*. In that moment—if the adult keeps still—the responsibility for the child's behavior falls squarely on the child's own shoulders. You wouldn't want it any other way.

When it comes to counting, your silence will speak louder than your words.

Our Famous Twinkie Example

Our famous Twinkie example will help you better understand the workings of the 1-2-3 program. This is a situation almost all parents have experienced at one time or another, and you may remember it from the beginning of the introduction to this book. Mom is cooking dinner at 5:45 p.m. when her eight-year-old daughter walks into the kitchen:

"Can I have a Twinkie?"
"No, dear."
"Why not?"
"Because we're eating at six o'clock."

Is there anything wrong with this conversation? No. The child asks a clear question and the parent gives a clear answer. The problem, however, is that some kids won't leave it there. They will press the issue further by adding in a whiny voice, "Yeah, but I want one."

What is this parent going to do now? She's a little aggravated and she's already given the necessary explanation. Should she repeat herself? Elaborate on her answer? Keep quiet? Give a reprimand?

Let's play this situation through in three scenes. In Scene I, we'll have a mother who believes that kids are little adults, and that words and reasons will work everything out. We'll see what happens with that approach.

Then, in Scene II, our mother will be getting smarter. She will be starting to use counting, but the child won't be used to it yet.

In Scene III, the mother will be using the 1-2-3 method, and her daughter will be used to the program and know how to respond to it.

SCENE I: STARRING THE MOTHER WHO BELIEVES KIDS ARE LITTLE ADULTS

"Can I have a Twinkie?"
"No, dear."
"Why not?"
"'Cause we're eating at six o'clock."
"Yeah, but I want one."

"I just said you couldn't have one."

"You never give me anything."

"What do you mean I never give you anything? Do you have clothes on? Is there a roof over your head? Am I feeding you in two seconds?"

"You gave Joey one half an hour ago."

"Listen, are you your brother? And besides, *he* eats his dinner."

"I promise I'll eat my dinner."

"Don't give me this promise, promise, promise stuff, Monica! Yesterday—at four thirty in the afternoon—you had half a peanut-butter-and-jelly sandwich, and you didn't eat anything at dinner!"

"THEN I'M GOING TO KILL MYSELF AND THEN RUN AWAY FROM HOME!"

"WELL, BE MY GUEST. I'M SICK OF THIS!"

You can see where trying to talk at the wrong time can get you. Though everything Mom said was true, her talking made the situation worse.

In the next scene, Mom is getting smarter and starting to use the 1-2-3 program, but it's new and the child is still getting used to it.

SCENE II: STARRING THE MOTHER BEGINNING THE 1-2-3 PROGRAM

"Can I have a Twinkie?"

"No, dear."

"Why not?"

"Because we're eating at six o'clock."

"Yeah, but I want one."

"That's 1."

"You never give me anything!"

"That's 2."

"THEN I'M GOING TO KILL MYSELF AND THEN RUN AWAY FROM HOME!"

"That's 3. Take five."

Mom did much better. The temporarily unhappy child disappears for a rest period, and the episode is over.

How's it going to go when the child is more used to counting and realizes that testing and manipulation are useless?

SCENE III: THE 1-2-3 AFTER THE CHILD IS USED TO COUNTING
"Can I have a Twinkie?"
"No, dear."
"Why not?"
"Because we're eating at six o'clock."
"Yeah, but I want one."
"That's 1."
(Pause.) "Oh, all right." (Grumpy exit from kitchen.)

Good work by Mom again. She doesn't have to count the grumpy "Oh, all right" because the comment is minor and the child is leaving the scene of the crime. If the child had said, "Oh, all right, you stupid jerk!" there would be an automatic 3 and the girl would be off to her room for a longer break.

Is ignoring the child's badgering an option? Perhaps, if (1) the child quickly gets the message and drops the issue and if (2) the parent can stand it. But in general—and especially in the beginning—counting is best.

The Benefits of Counting

There are a lot of benefits to using the 1-2-3 program to manage difficult childhood behavior. Here are just a few of them.

Energy Savings!
The 1-2-3 method will save you a lot of breath—and a lot of aggravation. Parents and teachers say counting makes discipline a whole lot less exhausting. Give one explanation, if absolutely necessary, and then count. No extra talking and no extra emotion. You stay calmer and you feel better—about your child and yourself—when you get a good response at 1 or 2.

When is an explanation or more talking absolutely necessary? In those instances when the problem involved is something new that the child does not understand, when his behavior was unusual or dangerous, or when you really need more information from him about what happened.

Here's an example. Your seven-year-old son has been learning trampoline in gym class and he loves it. After school he comes home, takes off his shoes, and attacks the couch in the living room. He's jumping up and down and trying to do flips. You enter the room, see what's going on, and are somewhat startled. You say, "That's 1." Your son says, "What did I do?"

> **Quik Tip**
> Give one explanation, if absolutely necessary, and then count. No extra talking and no extra emotion. You stay calmer and you feel better.

Is an explanation in order? Yes. He's never been trampolining on your couch before. You tell him that although he took off his shoes, which you appreciate, you're afraid he'll hurt himself or ruin the couch and that's why you counted. Good explanation.

When is an explanation not necessary? Imagine that a few hours later on the same day, the same seven-year-old—for no apparent reason—gives his younger sister a medium-sized shove right in front of you. You say, "That's 1." He growls, "WHAT DID I DO?" You say, "That's 2." This is pure defiance, not a real question. Do you need to explain that he just shoved his sister? Of course not. An explanation here would simply invite the boy to argue with you. And this kid sounds like he's ready for an argument! Argue back and you have just left the discipline ballpark again.

More Affection, More Fun

It's sad to say, but in many families, careless attempts at discipline take up lots and lots of time. The Talk-Persuade-Argue-Yell—and sometimes Hit—syndrome can run its course in less than a minute, but it can also occupy hours and hours. During this time everyone is agitated and angry. Parents do not like their kids, and kids do not like their parents.

With the 1-2-3 method, the issue is usually settled in a matter of seconds. Are the children frustrated when they are counted and don't get their way? Of course, but they get over it more quickly than they would if you and they spent an hour or so trying to persuade, argue, and yell each other into submission. After counting, things quickly go back to normal. You can enjoy your kids and they can enjoy you. There is not only more *time* for fun and affection, but you also *feel* more like having fun and being affectionate.

Your Authority Is Not Negotiable

You would go crazy if you had to negotiate—every day—issues like getting up, going to school, going to bed, homework, whining, and sibling rivalry. But you shouldn't have to, because you are the boss. As a matter of fact, as a parent you must frustrate your kids on a regular basis, because you can't possibly give them everything they want.

Many parents complicate their job of discipline by trying to be too nice. In other words, they set two goals for themselves instead of just one. Their first goal is to discipline their children, which is fine. But their second goal is *to get the kids to like it*! Like the mother in Scene I of the famous Twinkie example, the parents talk and talk and talk, waiting for the children to say something like, "Gee, I never looked at it like that before. Thanks for taking the time to explain it to me. I appreciate your efforts to raise me to be a responsible child."

Let's get real. There's the Little Adult Assumption lurking in the back of the parental brain again. If your child does listen all the time and more talking seems to help, fine. You're lucky. But with frustrated children that is not usually the case. Too often all that talking escalates to arguing and worse.

The Punishment Is Short and Sweet

The 1-2-3 Magic program is a control on the kids, but it's also a control on the parents. As a parent, it's not always easy to be reasonable, especially when you're angry. These days there is an argument about the use of punishment in raising kids. Some vote for no punishment at all; some vote for limited punishment; and, sadly, some parents are just plain brutal and take punishment too far.

I once spoke with a mother who was court-ordered to see me because she'd poured Drano down her four-year-old's throat once when the child talked back to her. I also knew a father who set fire to his daughter's doll in the kitchen sink (after dousing the thing with lighter fluid) after a long argument about homework. These are examples of cruel, unusual, and stupid punishments.

Though the vast majority of parents will never come close to taking such ridiculous and nasty measures, they may still be vulnerable to episodes of yelling, name-calling, belittling, or even rough physical tactics. But with 1-2-3 Magic the consequences are reasonable, well-defined, and just potent enough to do the job.

Are BreakTime and BreakTime alternatives punishments? In a way, yes. They are somewhat unpleasant. A rest period, though, is also a chance for everyone to calm down. These brief and reasonable consequences do not make the child so mad that he wants war. With this regimen, for example, most kids come back from BreakTime having forgotten about the whole thing. And you as the parent are not allowed to bring up and rehash what happened—unless absolutely necessary—so that also helps the house *quickly* return to normal.

So what's the bottom line? Is there a role for punishment in raising children? Yes, but mild, reasonable punishment administered by a non-tantruming parent.

Easy for Other Caretakers to Learn

The 1-2-3 program is easy enough to learn that you can train babysitters, grandparents, and other caregivers to use it. Parents who are using 1-2-3 at home often tell their child's teachers about the program. In turn, teachers who use 1-2-3 Magic in class often share the idea with parents who are struggling with their child's behavior at home.

When kids get the same message from everyone at home and at school, this cross-situational consistency makes the program much more powerful and easier for the children to learn. Whether at home or at school, "That's 1" means "You're doing something wrong, and it's time to shape up."

We have found that home-school coordination of the 1-2-3 program is especially helpful with behaviorally difficult children. When both parents and teachers use counting fairly and consistently, and when they also respect the No Talking and No Emotion Rules, we have seen positive changes take place in the behavior of some very challenging kids.

BreakTime Alternatives (BTAs)

For various reasons, there may be times when you do not want to use a BreakTime as the consequence for a child arriving at a count of 3. Perhaps there isn't time for a rest period when you're dashing out the door in the morning. Perhaps you feel you want a consequence with a little more clout, or perhaps you want a consequence that fits the crime. The judicious use of BreakTime alternatives can be of great value. Here are some BTA possibilities:

- Earlier bedtime
- No dessert or treat
- No use of phone
- No friend over
- No conversation—fifteen minutes
- Removal of DVD, iPod
- Reduced computer time

- Loss of TV for evening
- Loss of electronic games—two hours
- Monetary fine
- Small chore—wash bathroom sink
- Larger chore—weed yard
- Write a paragraph

Groundings, fines, chores, and losses like these can be very useful as consequences, and there are many other options. The list of BreakTime alternatives is limited only by your imagination. Remember to keep the punishments fair and reasonable. Your goal is to teach the child something, not to be cruel or get revenge.

Consequences can also be what some people call logical or natural, which means the punishment fits the misbehavior. Throwing a football in the house, for example, might result in the football being taken away. Or a count of 3 might mean the loss of an ice cream bar that was dripping on the car seat. The TV can be turned off if warnings to turn the volume down are ignored.

In applying natural consequences, remember that kids are still just kids. Exasperated lectures from you along the lines of "Well, this wouldn't have happened if you'd have simply listened to me in the first place" are unnecessary. Unnecessary conversation from you also interferes with your child's ability to appreciate the connection between his behavior and its consequences.

Remember, don't start counting your kids until you've read through the whole program and know the answers to any questions that might come up!

Counting Should Be Gentle, But Also Firm

Have you ever felt that your child's behavior is like a car racing out of control? When you count calmly, decisively, and gently, you are helping your child stop and change direction. That's a hard thing for their young brain to accomplish! When you count properly, it's like you're directly wiring the neurons in their brain correctly and helping them push that brake pedal. Over time, after you have repeatedly connected those neurons in that way, your child will follow the brain road you have created for them.

If, on the other hand, you count with excessive anger, you are actually challenging your child to misbehave. Their brain will send the "fight" signal, and they'll forget temporarily that they do want to get along with you. At the other extreme, if you count with a voice that is anxious, pleading, and whimpering, the kids will immediately sense that you don't know what you're doing. They will become angry as well as frightened (am I—a kid—in charge of this house?!), and their behavior will be chaotic.

CHAPTER SUMMARY

At this point, you're almost ready to start counting, but in the back of your mind, you probably have a few questions. What if the kids won't go to BreakTime? What if they won't stay? What if they tantrum constantly during their "rest period"? To be effective with counting, you need to be calm and decisive. To be calm and decisive, you need to know the answers not only to these questions, but also to many of the other questions parents often ask about the procedure. We'll deal with this list of FAQs in the next chapter.

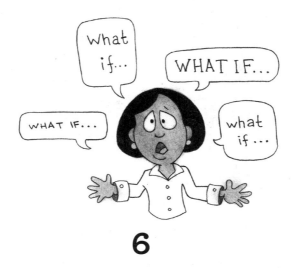

6
ADVICE FOR NEARLY ANY COUNTING CHALLENGE

Answers to Our Most Frequently Asked Questions

1-2-3 MAGIC'S COUNTING STRATEGY is straightforward, but managing kids' irritating behavior is never an easy job. At this point you probably have a number of questions about this first big phase of parenting. Let's take a look at some of the most frequently asked ones.

What if the child won't go to BreakTime?
If the child won't go to his room after hitting a count of 3, remember you are not allowed to use Little Adult attempts at persuasion, such as, "Come on now, do what Dad told you. It's only for five minutes, and then you'll be able to go back and play. I'm not asking a lot…" And so on, and so on. What you do instead depends on how big you are and how big the child is.

The little kids: Let's say you weigh one hundred twenty-five pounds, and your five-year-old son weighs forty-five pounds. If he doesn't go to his room at 3, you simply move toward him. Some kids will then stay two feet ahead of you all the way to the room. That's OK; they'll soon start going by themselves. Other kids have to be "escorted" (keep your mouth closed while doing this), which can mean taking them gently by the arm, as well as dragging or carrying them to the room.

The bigger kids: Now let's imagine that it's five years later. Your ten-year-old son at this point weighs ninety-five pounds, and you—through a rigid program of diet and exercise—still weigh one hundred twenty-five. You are no longer in a position to get into a physical altercation with this boy. He's too big, and wrestling matches make a fool out of you.

Your savior here will be the BreakTime alternative. If after your "That's 3. Take ten," your son doesn't appear to be going anywhere, you inform him that he has a choice. He can go for a break or choose one of the following: bedtime half an hour earlier, fifty cents off his allowance, or no electronic entertainment for the evening. "Community service," some kind of small chore, is also a nice option. (Some parents have used weeding or scrubbing a sink or toilet.) Many parents let the child pick the consequence. If the child refuses, the parent selects the punishment.

A problem arises here because your child hasn't gone to his room and the two of you are still face-to-face. Lots of kids in this situation want to stick around and argue with you about how stupid your rules are, how stupid 1-2-3 Magic is, and how stupid the guy who wrote it must be.

You know you're not allowed to argue. What are you going to do? You can use a "reverse BreakTime," in which *you* just turn around and leave the room. Go to your room or even the bathroom if necessary—having stocked them with good reading materials beforehand—and wait the storm out. Or walk around the house a few times. But don't talk.

Some parents have asked, "Why should I be the one to leave? After all, I'm the adult." Fine. Stay put if you can keep quiet and avoid both being provocative and being provoked. But if your real motive is the desire to stick around for a good fight, that's a bad strategy.

Can you count different misbehaviors to get to three?

Yes. You don't have to have different counts for each different kind of misbehavior. Imagine: "Let's see, he's on a 1 for throwing that block across the room. He's on a 2 for teasing his sister. He's on a 1 for yelling at me. He's on a 2 for..."

This routine would soon drive you insane, and you'd need to use your computer to keep track of everything. So if the child pushes his sister, for example, "That's 1." If he throws a block across the room, "That's 2," and then if he screams at you for counting him, "That's 3. Take five." Mom could say "1," Dad could say "2," and Mom or Dad could say, "That's 3." In fact, we encourage you to share the joy.

Actually, it's better if Mom and Dad *do* both count, because then the kids know that both parents are behind the plan—they are consistent and really serious. The involvement of both parents makes it easier for the children to shape up. In the same way, the involvement of both home and school in doing the 1-2-3 method also makes it easier for kids to behave—especially the really difficult children.

> **Quik Tip**
> What if the child won't take a rest period? It's OK to "escort" little kids to the chair or room. That could mean carrying them, but you must keep quiet! Switch older kids to a BreakTime alternative. Give them a choice or decide yourself, then walk away.

Can you ever ignore anything? Introducing the MBA!

How do you know when you should count? Usually it's not too difficult to tell. Most of the time, if you're irritated about something and that something is a Stop behavior, you should be counting. Just to be sure, you and your kids can write a list of countable behaviors.

However, there can be times when you're irritated but the kids are not really misbehaving and you should not count. We call these activities "MBAs," Minor But Aggravating actions that may rub you the wrong way but are not really misbehavior. Humming, singing the same song over and over, rolling the eyes and stomping to BreakTime, squirminess, chasing the dog, and eating all the frosting off the top of the cupcake first may be examples. If the child's not really misbehaving and you're just in a bad mood, the best thing to do is grit your teeth and keep quiet.

The question of ignoring certain types of behavior leaves room for some variation among parents. Why? Because some parents simply have longer fuses than others. Some parents, for example, will ignore kids' rolling their eyes, stomping off, grumbling, and whining, while other parents will count. Some parents will ignore a child's yelling or even pounding walls as long as he's on his way to a rest period. Other parents will lengthen the rest period for that kind of behavior. Either strategy is correct if it is done consistently. You have to clearly define what kinds of child behavior, in your well-considered opinion, are too obnoxious, too rude, too aggressive, or too dangerous. Then make up your mind that those behaviors are the ones that will be counted.

> **Caution**
> Your kids already have their MBAs! Minor But Aggravating actions that may rub you the wrong way but which are not really misbehavior. These may include humming, squirminess, rolling the eyes, and eating the frosting off the top of the cupcake first.

But in the beginning with 1-2-3 Magic, don't ignore genuine misbehavior. In the beginning, when in doubt, count! After a while, when you're getting a good response at 1 or 2, you may be able to let up a little.

Let's say, for example, that after a few weeks getting used to the 1-2-3 program, your child does something right in front of you that would normally be counted. Instead of counting right away, just watch your kid. The child can almost "feel" the count coming. Sometimes, if you say nothing, the child will spontaneously exercise self-control and stop the misbehavior. This response is ideal, because now the child is internalizing the rules and controlling himself without direct parental intervention. Isn't that the kind of person you want to drop off at the dorm on the first day of his freshman year in college?

How long do you take in between counts?

About five seconds. Just long enough to allow the child time to shape up. Remember that we're counting Stop (obnoxious) behaviors, such as arguing, whining, badgering, and teasing. It only takes a child one second to cooperate with you by stopping the annoying activity. We certainly don't want to give a child half an hour to continue a tantrum before giving him a 2.

Counting is perfectly designed to produce the one second of motivation necessary for cooperation. We give the kids five seconds, though, which is a little more generous. Why five seconds? Because this brief pause gives the children time to think things over and do the right thing. In those few seconds—provided the adult keeps quiet—kids learn to take responsibility for their own behavior.

If a child hits a 1 or a 2, does he stay at that count for the rest of the day, even if he does nothing else wrong?

No. The time perspective of young children is short. You would not say "That's 1" at nine in the morning, "That's 2" at eleven fifteen, and "That's 3. Take five" at three in the afternoon. We have what we call our "window of opportunity" rule. For example, if a six-year-old does three things wrong in a thirty-minute period, each warning counts toward the total of three. But if he does one thing wrong, then an hour goes by, then he does something else he shouldn't, you can start back at 1.

Very few children manipulate this rule by doing one thing, allowing thirty minutes to pass, and then figuring, "Now I get a free one!" If you feel your child is trying to get away with this, simply make the next count a 2 instead of going back to 1.

The window of opportunity should be longer as kids get older. Here is a general guideline: for four-year-olds, consider a time period of ten or fifteen minutes; for eleven-year-olds, think about two to three hours. Classroom teachers in the primary grades do not usually use a short window because, with twenty-five children in the class, this would allow for too much potential misbehavior in too short a time. Instead, the counting period in school is expanded to cover the entire morning. All counts are washed away at lunchtime, and then the afternoon is treated as a new and separate window.

Can you use a BreakTime chair instead of a room?

You can use a stair or a chair for a rest period, but only if the child does not make a game out of the situation. Some kids, for example, sit on the chair at first, but then start gradually losing contact with it. Eventually they may just be touching their little finger to the chair and looking at you like, "What are you going to do about this?"

If your rule for BreakTime is simply that the child must stay in contact with the chair, this is no problem. But if the child is getting on and off or away from the chair and you're uncertain what to do, this kind of game will ruin the discipline.

We usually prefer that visual contact between parent and child be broken during the rest period, so the child can't tease or provoke you. That's why the child's bedroom or other safe room is preferable. However, many parents have successfully used stairs and chairs, and many report that the kids—even some wild ones!—sit still on them, don't talk, and don't keep getting off. As a matter of fact, parents are often very creative in coming up with places for rest periods.

> **Key Concept**
> The main point is this: it is totally unproductive and harmful to be chasing the kids back into the room all the time. The child needs to know that there is a barrier that she is stuck with for a short period of time.

What if the child won't stay in his room?

Many kids will stay in the room for the BreakTime, even if the door isn't shut. Others, however, will keep coming out. With very small children, one alternative is to just stand there blocking the way or to hold the door shut. After a few breaks, the kids get the idea that they can't come out. This tactic won't work, however, if you keep getting into major tugs of war with the door. If your discipline comes down to this level, you look stupid.

A second alternative is to block the child's exit with the kind of gate that squeezes against the doorjambs. These gates can be used as long as the children are not able to either climb over or knock down the device. Yet another option is to start BreakTime over if the child comes out prematurely. Some parents will then double the time of the second rest period. This method, of course, won't be much help with two- or three-year-olds because they won't understand, but with older children it can work well. Explain once and then start.

Some kids, however, are so rambunctious that they just keep coming out and accumulate what seem like thousands of extra BreakTime minutes. What should you do? You need to secure the door in some way or another. There are several options.

Believe it or not, some parents of difficult children have made the child's bedroom door into a "Dutch" door. They saw the door in half, then lock the bottom part and leave the top part open during BreakTime. You may think that's a fairly drastic solution. It is, but some kids require drastic (but gentle) solutions.

Also available are plastic doorknob covers. These devices cover the knob and have to be squeezed tightly to turn the knob and open the door. Many young children aren't strong enough to accomplish this.

Another idea is to simply put some kind of lock on the door. This advice worries some parents who think that their child will become claustrophobic or that locking the door is abusive. Locking the door for a short time is not by itself abusive, but for some groups (for example, foster parents) and in some places (for example, some provinces of Canada) it is illegal. If you have a really difficult child, you should check what regulations apply to your situation and get some professional advice.

Here's an option for locking the door. You tell your child that as long as he stays in his room, the door will remain open or simply shut. But the first time he comes out, the door gets locked for the rest period. Many children will quickly learn to stay put without the door having to be locked. If you still prefer gates to locks, purchase one of the more solid gates that bolts into the doorjambs. If the child can climb over the gate, get a taller one or put two up.

The main point is this: some children will try to keep coming out of the room. If so, securing the door in some way is absolutely essential. It is totally unproductive and harmful to be chasing the kids back into the room all the time. The child must know that the door is a barrier that he's stuck with for a short time. Once children learn they can't get out of the room, they will stop their tantrums and calmly accept the brief period of quiet.

If you worry about the safety of the child, childproof the room, secure any windows, and remain outside the door during BreakTime—but try not to let the child know you're there. If you still feel the child is not safe alone in the room or if you feel he would suffer excessive separation anxiety, you may go in the room during the rest period. But no eye contact and no talking!

And don't forget the one-minute-per-year rule for the length of the rest period. Remember that you may not increase the length of the break simply because you're in a bad mood. You can increase the length of BreakTime—to a point—if the child did something that is exceptionally bad.

What if the child tantrums during BreakTime?

For children four and older, the BreakTime does not start until they're done with their tantrum. Explain this only once to the child. So if they scream and yell for fifty minutes, the rest period starts after fifty minutes. It's important to leave them alone during their tantrum—telling them to quiet down will only make them worse.

For kids three and younger who tantrum, let them out after their time is up, even if they are still tantruming. Walk away and say nothing. A discussion at this point will be throwing gasoline on the fire. If the child quiets down, fine. If they continue to tantrum after they are out, count them again. If they arrive at three, they go back to BreakTime and you can double the time.

What do you do if the child counts you back?

Your five-year-old is whining at you because you wouldn't take her to the pool on a hot summer day. You look at her, hold up one finger, and say, "That's 1." She looks back at you, holds up one tiny finger, and says, "That's 1 to you too!"

What should you do? Oddly enough, this common occurrence sometimes throws even the most confident parents for a loop. They are at a loss on how to handle the unexpected rebellion. Some parents have even said, "1-2-3 Magic doesn't work—the kid just counts me back!"

So what do you do? Your kids do not have the authority to count anyone (unless you give that power to them). The child might as well have said, "The moon is made of cream cheese." The comment itself means nothing—but it might be a countable misbehavior.

Here's how you decide. If the child's remark appears to be a humorous attempt to tease you a little, you can just ignore it. But if her "That's 1 to you too!" is sarcastic and disrespectful, count it by simply holding up two fingers and saying nothing. If the child again mocks your response, she will have just arrived at 3. Send her to BreakTime and repeat as necessary.

Can one of your kids count another one? Generally no. The only time this can occur is if one child is old enough to babysit the other. But make sure to get a report when you come back.

Does the room have to be a sterile environment?

No. Many parenting books tell you the rest period room should be modeled after a cell in a state penitentiary. Complete and utter boredom—that'll teach 'em! This is unnecessary. The child can go to her room and read, take a nap, play with Legos, draw, and so on. Just to be safe, though, three things should be forbidden: no phone, no friends, and no electronic entertainment.

Some people ask: "Well then, just how is a rest period supposed to work? My kid tells me that BreakTime is fine with her. She doesn't care, and she'll just go upstairs and play." Don't pay much attention to any child who says, "I don't care." That comment usually means the opposite: she does care. And if her room were such a great place to be, she would have been up there in the first place.

The fact of the matter is that the power of the 1-2-3 method does not come so much from the rest period itself. It usually comes from the interruption of the child's activities. When this girl was timed out for hitting her brother, she was watching her favorite TV show. Now she has to miss a big chunk of the show. No one—including you—likes to be interrupted and miss out on something fun.

If you really feel the BreakTime strategy is not effective, consider three things. First, are you still talking too much and getting too emotional during discipline efforts? Parental outbursts ruin everything. Second, if you feel you are remaining calm and BreakTime is still not working, consider another rest period place or room. Third, consider BreakTime alternatives.

Why three counts? Children should respond the first time you ask! Why give the kids three chances to misbehave?

It's interesting to hear different parents' reactions to 1-2-3 Magic. Some people (usually those attempting to discipline their children for the first time) think counting is too dictatorial, while others see counting as a sign of parental weakness, believing that children shouldn't get three chances to misbehave before being punished.

The reason for three counts is simple. You want to give the kids two chances—the first two counts—to shape up (unless what they did was so serious that it merited an automatic 3). How are children going to learn to do the right thing if they never get a chance? And with counting, the "chance" comes right away—in the first few seconds following the count. That immediate opportunity helps them learn. They're just kids!

What if you have other people over?

By this time, you can probably anticipate the answer to this question. You will need to (1) get used to counting in front of other people and (2) not alter your strategy one bit when others are watching. The ultimate test, of course, is when you're out in public (see next chapter). For right now, we'll discuss what should happen in the safety of your own home.

From time to time, other people will be at your home when your kids decide to act up. In fact, the presence of other people often seems to trigger disruptive behavior in many kids, presenting parents with the complicated challenge of disciplining children while on stage. Among the groups of people who perversely decide to put you in this awkward position are your children's friends, other parents (with or without their kids), and finally, grandparents. Let's examine the problems presented by each group.

Other Kids: If your child has a friend over, count your child just as you would if no one else were there. If your child gets timed out, he goes to the room and—remember—his friend may not join him. Just explain to the other boy or girl that you're using this new system and your child will be back in five minutes or so. If your son or daughter says to you, "Mom, it's so embarrassing when you count me in front of my friends," you say to them once, "If you don't want to be embarrassed, you can behave."

Another thing you can do in this situation is count the other child too. After all, it's your house. If his parent is there, you'd better ask permission and explain a bit before you start disciplining her child.

Another variation with other kids over is "1-2-3, 1-2-3, 1-2-3: out of the house to play." This can be very helpful, especially if you have a difficult child who often gets overly excited when a playmate is over. With this routine, at the point where the third BreakTime would be assigned, instead of sending your child to the room again, both kids must now leave the house for a specified time (assuming the weather isn't nasty) and play outside. This variation of the 1-2-3 is very popular in southern California.

> **Quik Tip**
> If your child looks at you and says, "It's so embarrassing when you count me in front of my friends!" you simply reply, "If you don't want to be embarrassed, you can behave."

Or—even better—1-2-3, 1-2-3, 1-2-3, then send them over to the other kid's house to play. I've done it!

Other adults: If you have other adults over at your home, you will probably feel considerably more nervous counting your child. This discomfort is normal. Although you may feel a little self-conscious at first, you'll soon get used to doing the 1-2-3 method under these circumstances. So count! If you don't take the plunge, your children will sense that you are much easier prey when other people are around.

On the other hand, when you count in front of another parent, something surprising may happen that you will enjoy. For example, imagine you're talking to a friend and your child rudely and loudly interrupts you demanding a snack. You calmly say, "That's 1." Your child not only quiets down, but she also leaves the room. The other parent looks at you like, "What did you do?" Just tell her about 1-2-3 Magic and explain how it works. This scene shows one of the major ways that 1-2-3 Magic gets passed around.

Grandparents: For our purposes here, there are three types of grandparents, whether you're visiting them or they're visiting you. The first—and rarest—type of grandparent is the *cooperative* grandparent. She will count along with you. You say 1, Grandma says 2, and so on. That kind of cooperation is super, but it doesn't happen as much as we'd like.

Like the first type, the second type of grandparent is also nice to have around. This person we call the *passive* or *nonintrusive* grandparent. This grandma or grandpa leaves you alone when you're disciplining the kids and doesn't interfere. That's often not easy for a grandparent.

The third type of grandparent, however, is the *antagonistic* grandparent. He will say something to you like this: "You have to read a book to learn how to raise your kids? Why, when I was a boy, all Dad had to do was look at his belt." You know the rest. The message is that you don't need any of this modern psychological stuff.

A second kind of antagonistic grandparent will actually interfere with your discipline. You say to little Bobby, "That's 3. Take five," and before he can move, Grandma butts in and says, "Oh, little Bobby didn't really do anything. Bobby, come and sit on Grandma's lap for a while."

Some parents ask at this point: "Can you count the grandparents?" Probably not, but you do have an assertiveness problem on your hands. You may have to say something like, "You know, Mom, I love you very much, but these are our kids and this is the way we're raising them. If you can't go along with the agenda, the visit may have to be cut short a little." Although this statement will be a very difficult one to make, the comment will definitely be an investment in your children's future.

What if the child won't come out from BreakTime?

You probably know the answer to this one. Relax and enjoy yourself! You go to the bedroom door and say, "Time's up." Your son or daughter replies, "I'm never coming out again as long as I live!" Don't say, "Good!" or anything like that. Just walk away—never chase a martyr.

On the other hand, do not cheat by extending the break. Imagine your child's rest period was for five minutes. You just noticed, though, that you got distracted and eight minutes elapsed. You think, "Oh, it's so peaceful! And she's being so quiet in her room! Why let her out?" Wrong—no fair. Keep an eye on the clock or timer, then tell the child when the time is up. If your girl has fallen asleep—and if it's OK for her to nap at this time of day—let her snooze for a bit.

Some kids always want a hug and some reassurance when BreakTime is over. What do you do? Give them a hug! But be careful with these little huggers. If a child repeatedly requests a hug, you'd better check to make sure you're using the program correctly. Some kids are just very sensitive and any kind of discipline upsets them a little. Other children need reassurance because you were too harsh—emotionally or physically—before you sent them to the room. So if you get a little hugger, make sure you're gently following the No Talking and No Emotion Rules.

Help—my kids go nuts when I'm on the phone!

This problem brings back vivid memories to all parents. It seems that all parents have experienced their child acting up when the parents are on the phone. The ringing seems to be the signal that it's time to cut loose!

At our house, the dog would also get into the act. The phone would ring and the dog would bark. The dog's bark was a signal to the kids: "We've got another victim on the line, get down here and let's torture him for a while!" Then they'd all be running around, yelling and barking and having a wonderful time. Whoever was on the phone would feel trapped and frustrated.

Why do children always seem to act up when you're on the phone? At first I thought it was because the kids were jealous of the parent talking to someone else and ignoring them. This may be partly true, but now I believe the main reason is that the children think you are *helpless*. The kids seem to believe that since your head is attached to the phone, you won't be able to do anything to counter them raising a ruckus.

> **Quik Tip**
> Why do kids always seem to act up whenever you're on the phone? It's probably because they think you are helpless. Let them know you're not by counting just as you would if you weren't talking to someone.

The best thing to do is count the children just as you would if you weren't on the phone—much like when you have other people over. While you're on the phone you have somebody else present—but only listening, not watching. You may have to interrupt your conversation to count. You may have to put the phone down or explain what you're doing to the person you're talking to, or even hang up so you can escort a little one to her room. Some calls become more expensive, but whatever it takes, do it. Otherwise the children will know that you are a sitting duck every time someone calls.

This phone routine is not easy in the beginning. After a while, though, many parents succeed in training the children to the point that the adults don't have to say anything while counting. They simply hold up the appropriate number of fingers while they continue their conversation! And the children respond because they know Mom or Dad means business. If you've gotten to this point, it's a mighty handy tactic to use when you're talking on the telephone.

What if the kid wrecks the room during his so-called "rest period"?

The vast majority of children will not be room wreckers. Only a small percentage of kids will throw things around and mess up the room. An even smaller percentage of children will break things, tear their beds apart, or kick holes in the wall. Their parents need to know how to handle these sometimes scary actions.

The point behind 1-2-3 Magic is that parents be ready for anything, rather than feeling defensive and worrying, "Oh no, what is he going to do now?" We want your attitude and message to the children to be something like this: "You're my child and I'm your parent. I love you, and it's my job to train and discipline you. I don't expect you to be perfect, and when you do something wrong, this is what I will do."

The credit for the solution to the room-wrecking problem comes from a couple who visited my office a long time ago. They had an eight-year-old boy who was very nice to me in my office, but—according to his mom and dad—was "hell on wheels" everywhere else. These parents said they were thinking of putting this boy's name on their mailbox, because it felt like he was running the house. They often referred to their son as "King Louis XIV."

This behavior obviously couldn't go on, so I asked these parents if they wanted to learn 1-2-3 Magic. They said yes. I taught them the program, prepared them for testing and manipulation, and they went home to get started. This boy had been used to running the house, but when his parents got home they were ready for him.

> **Key Concept**
> The point behind 1-2-3 Magic is that parents are ready for anything, rather than worrying what the kids are going to do next. The message is: "I love you, and it's my job to train and discipline you. I don't expect you to be perfect, and when you act up, this is what I will do."

When King Louis hit 3 for the first time, he could not believe what happened. How his parents got him to his room for his first rest period is still a mystery, but when he got there, he totally—and

I mean totally—trashed the place. His first tactic, and perhaps the favorite of all room wreckers, was to empty his dresser and throw his clothes all over the floor. Then he ripped the blankets and sheets off his bed. Next he pushed the mattress and box spring off the bed frame. Then he proceeded to his closet, took out all his hanging clothes, and threw them all over the room. After that, he tossed all his toys out of the closet. Finally, he went to the window and tore down his curtains.

What did his parents do? Amazingly, they didn't call me for help. The first thing they did was nothing! They didn't clean up the mess or have King Louis clean it up. Any cleaning up would have meant loading the boy's gun again for the next rest period when he'd have another perfectly neat room to wreck. Second, Mom and Dad continued to count their son aggressively but fairly.

> **Quik Tip**
> If your child wrecks her room during a tantrum, one option is for you to ignore the mess and let her live in it for a few days! That might make the child think twice before doing it again.

When the boy earned a 3, he got a 3 and a consequence. No fudging around with fractions such as, "That's 2 and a half, that's 2 and three-quarters." The parents would hit him with his well-earned 3 and then send him to his bedroom to rearrange the trash. When bedtime came, this boy had to find his pajamas. He also had to find his bed. In the mornings, his clothes for school didn't match for a week.

How long did it take for King Louis to learn that there was new management in the old *maison*? It took about ten days for him to start calming down during breaks. Then, after three or four days of peaceful BreakTimes, his parents helped him clean up his room. After that—believe it or not—he hated to be counted, and his parents would stop him on a dime with a count of 1.

Now, did we break this boy's spirit? Was he going to be a marshmallow for the rest of his life? Certainly not. Now he was really and consistently the nice kid I had seen in the office, and his parents were in charge of their own house—as they should have been from the beginning. In addition, the boy started behaving better in school, where the teacher was also using the 1-2-3 program.

If you think you are going to have a room wrecker, before starting 1-2-3 Magic, check out two things. If there is anything dangerous or harmful in the room, or anything valuable that can be broken, take it out before the first rest period.

Room wrecking is one thing, but what do you do if your child urinates on the floor during rest periods?

Some kids have done it—usually preschoolers. You send them to BreakTime, and they are so mad that they pull down their pants and cut loose. What do you do? You time them out to the bathroom.

I know what you're thinking: "How naive! Do you really expect the child to use the facilities appropriately?" The answer is no, but that's not the point. The point is this: What's easier to clean, the bedroom rug or the bathroom floor? If the child goes on the bedroom rug, cleaning is an expensive project. If the child goes on the bathroom floor or the smaller bathroom rug, it's a different story.

The same advice holds true if you have a child who can get himself so upset that he throws up. In every workshop I've ever done, a few parents have kids like this. Make sure the bathroom's safe, then time him out to the bathroom. And stay cool!

While we're on the subject, can you use counting for toilet training?

No. Counting is not especially effective for potty training. One reason is that if you are trying to count for children messing in their pants, you don't always know the exact moment when the "accident" occurs, so you don't know just when to count. In addition, most experts agree that punishing kids for wetting or soiling is not particularly helpful.

Though there are several effective ways to get kids to go on the toilet, my favorite method is for the parent to do very little formal training. Too many parents are in too big a hurry to get their kids potty trained, and this big rush can cause all kinds of trouble. Instead, let the kids see you use the toilet and get them a potty chair of their own. Most children will eventually learn how to use the thing without much direct coaching from you. When they are successful, you can then praise and reward them.

Another frequently unsuccessful parent tactic in this regard is repeatedly asking a child—when he's looking squirmy—if he has to go to the bathroom. It's much better to say this: "Someday you're gonna surprise me and go on the potty!"

What if there's an obvious problem between two of your children, but you didn't see what happened?

Your daughter, Suzie, comes running into the kitchen and yells, "Dad, Bobby should get a 1!" You haven't the slightest idea what the problem is, but the chances are the issue revolves around sibling rivalry. In general our rule is this: if you didn't see the argument or conflict, you don't count it. If you hear it, you can count it.

If you're in the kitchen and you hear a ruckus starting in the family room, for example, there's nothing to stop you from calling, "Hey, guys, that's 1." Of course, you want to use this rule with flexibility. If you feel one child is consistently being victimized by another, you may have to intervene and count just the aggressive child. On the other hand, if the tattling is getting out of hand, many parents decide to count the tattler.

Does being counted hurt the child's self-esteem?

Most kids aren't counted a lot, so the mere quantity of counts is usually not a problem. Once you've gotten started at home, many children will not get any counts for days at a time. In a regular classroom, on an average day, fewer than five children will get any count at all.

For those children who do get counted more often, if you are doing the 1-2-3 program correctly, there should be no significant threat of hurting self-esteem. What *will* hurt children's self-esteem is the yelling, arguing, name-calling, sarcasm, or hitting you may do if you don't control yourself. In addition, as you will see later, your overall feedback to your children should be much more positive than negative. And one count is a bit of negative feedback. Therefore, you will want to more than balance your occasional counting with other activities or strategies, such as affection, shared fun, listening, and praise.

Should you ever spank a child?

It's about time that people face up to reality: *the vast majority of spankings are parental temper tantrums*. They are in no way attempts to train or educate a child. They are simply the angry outbursts of a parent who has lost control, doesn't know what to do, and wants revenge by inflicting pain. Parents who have big problems with self-control and anger management try to justify and rationalize spanking by saying things like, "You have to set limits," "It's for their own good," and "Having to hit the kids hurts me more than it does them."

There are cultures and groups in which spanking is perceived as a legitimate discipline technique. There are also people who really do see—and use—spanking as a training device. But research suggests that *excessive* physical discipline tends to generate anxiety in children, lower their self-esteem, and make them more likely to become aggressive themselves.

Generally speaking, though, adults who spank do not care one bit about research. I have on occasion talked until I'm blue in the face with parents like these, and sadly enough, changing their opinions and their discipline habits is often a lost cause. Remember, the whole point of the 1-2-3 program is to avoid the Talk-Persuade-Argue-Yell-Hit routine.

My child has a fit when I try to drop him off at preschool. No matter how much I try to reassure him, he screams whenever I try to leave.

Though separation anxiety is normal in little children, the kids' desperate screams when you try to leave them at preschool, with a sitter, or even at Grandma's can be very upsetting to you. Here's what you do. Bite your lip and become the Master of the Quick Exit. When dropping children off (or leaving home), kiss the kids good-bye, tell them when you'll see them again, and get out of there! The longer you stay and the more you talk, the worse you will make the situation.

If these awful moments make you feel like a totally cold and uncaring parent, call back later and ask the caregiver how long your child cried. The average is eighty seconds.

Shouldn't the kids ever apologize?

This is a tough question. If you're currently asking your kids to apologize and that routine is working well, that's fine. Keep in mind, however, that many apologies are really exercises in hypocrisy. Requiring an apology is often simply part of the child's punishment—not a learning experience involving sorrow or compassion.

For example, imagine your two sons have gotten into a fight. You break up the tussle, then demand that they apologize to each another. The older boy glares at the younger and with a sneer on his face says, "I'm sorry." His tone is forced, begrudging, and sarcastic.

Now let me ask you two questions about this child's response. First, was this a real apology? Of course not. His comment was merely a continuation of the original battle, but on a verbal level. Second, was his statement a lie? The answer is yes. If you want to insist on apologies, make sure that you are not simply asking your children to lie.

Caution

Poor grades are not really misbehavior. And punishment for poor grades is a strategy that is way more often unsuccessful than useful. Try a friendly reward system first, and if that doesn't work, consider a professional evaluation.

What if my boy or girl misbehaves at school?

The first time this happens, ask your child to explain. Don't "double punish" the child if the teacher already took disciplinary action. Depending on the severity of the incident, you may want to talk to the teacher. Some problems vanish without a lot of effort on your part.

The second time your child misbehaves at school, you will want to talk to the teacher, possibly even with your child present. Though you may still decide to not take action, if the behavior continues you will want to work out a daily or weekly behavior chart (see charting in chapter 12) that the teacher fills out and sends home to keep you up to date. You may decide to link this chart to rewards and consequences that you administer at home. If this intervention doesn't succeed after a few weeks, try modifying your rewards, consequences, or the chart itself. If that doesn't work after a few more weeks, consider a professional evaluation through the school or privately.

One note of caution: poor grades are not really an incidence of misbehavior. And punishment-only methods for dealing with poor grades usually fail. Instead, use the system described earlier.

What about the 1-2-3 program and special-needs kids?

1-2-3 Magic can be used with typically developing kids or special-needs kids, such as children with ADHD, learning disabilities, oppositional defiant disorder, depression, and even autism spectrum disorders. The main requirement is that the child have a mental age of at least two.

Usually the counting method doesn't require much modification, but two special instances, both involving anxiety, should be mentioned. First, some children seem to become more anxious (not angry, but anxious) when they are verbally counted. Sometimes using a visual stimulus such as three cards (green = 1, yellow = 2, red = 3) is helpful.

Second, it is not helpful to count if the problem is anxiety. Anxiety, after all, is not willful misbehavior. A child who screams at the sight of a mosquito or who bellows furiously when you try to leave her at school will be better handled with reassurance and gentle but firm structure.

When should you talk?

Is a teachable moment the time immediately following BreakTime? The answer is no. The reason is this: a rest period is not only a consequence but also a cooling-off period. If you greet your child right after their rest period with a comment like, "Tell me what you did and how you're going to prevent future examples of this kind of behavior," you are likely to irritate the child. The cooling-off effect is lost, and you are not off to a nice, fresh start. If you insist on talking to your kids about an incident that occurred, do it some other time. Consider making an appointment, and use the tactics described in chapter 22.

I like the program. How do I get my husband involved?
Husbands are sometimes difficult to get onboard with systematic parenting programs. Here's what you do. Get a copy of the first (blue) DVD, *1-2-3 Magic: Managing Difficult Behavior*, which covers the program through approximately chapter 11 of this book. It may be available at your local library. Ask your husband to watch it. But there's a catch. You can't be in the room with him, because you may have a tendency to say, "See, this is what you need to be doing." That will turn him off for sure. If he's willing to cooperate after he watches the DVD, get started and later add Parenting Jobs 2 and 3 (purple DVD, *More 1-2-3 Magic*, or chapters 12–24 of this book). Using *1-2-3 Magic* with the kids is good for marriages!

Know What You're Doing!

Kids' brains don't need a magnifying glass to detect whether you know what you're doing in any given discipline situation. At these times, kids often respond emotionally. They may throw a tantrum, yell and scream, or cry and pout.

Unfortunately, parents can use these unhealthy tactics too. Especially if, when our children push our buttons, we don't have a strategy for responding. These emotional reactions clog the front of our brain and make it impossible for us to think. They also model poor emotional control for our kids.

By using the *1-2-3 Magic* strategy and by knowing the answers to *all* the FAQs in this chapter, your adult brain is able to provide a good automatic response to your child, thereby reducing your need to react emotionally.

CHAPTER SUMMARY

Long story short, we have an answer for any counting problem you might encounter!

Have we taken care of all possible questions?

Not quite. The most commonly asked question needs a whole chapter of explanation:

What do you do in public?

7

DISCIPLINING YOUR CHILD IN PUBLIC

How to Handle Grocery Store Meltdowns and Other Embarrassing Situations

WE NOW MUST COME to grips with the worst nightmare of every parent: what to do when your child misbehaves in public. No one wants to look like a child abuser in the candy aisle of the local grocery store. And kids—even very young toddlers—seem to have automatic radar that can sense psychological vulnerability in anxious parents.

Once they have learned the mechanics of the 1-2-3 program, many parents worry about being in public where there is no BreakTime room. The good news is this problem can be solved without too much difficulty. The bad news is that a worse problem is lurking in the shadows, and deep in her heart every parent knows what that problem is.

Your biggest problem in public is that your little ones can hold something over your head that they can't in private: the *threat of public embarrassment*. This fear of embarrassment and public disapproval has at times made even the most competent parents forget what they're supposed to do, abandon tried-and-true tactics, and crumble. Try to remember this basic principle: the long-term welfare of your kids comes before short-term worries about what others are going to think of you.

Counting in Public

Let's imagine that you have a five-year-old and that yes, in fact, the candy aisle in the grocery store is one of your biggest problems. It seems as though every time you go down that aisle, your son asks for candy. You say no, and then the little boy proceeds to throw a ferocious tantrum. He throws himself on the floor, screams at the top of his lungs, and—don't you love this part?—a crowd has gathered to see how you're going to handle the crisis.

What do you do? The first thing is to make sure you have the 1-2-3 program rolling fairly well at home. "Fairly well" means you are getting a good response at 1 or 2 most of the time. Now you're in aisle 5, your son is howling, and the audience has assembled. You look down at the unhappy little monster, hold up one finger, and say, "That's 1." You say this as calmly and as firmly as you would at home.

What is the key here? It's not so much what you say as what you don't say. You do not, for example, let yourself be intimidated by the threat of public embarrassment and whisper, "Come on now, I don't want you making a fool of me in front of all these people." If you do that, your child will *know* that you can be had for a nickel. He won't need the candy bar because he's about to have more fun with you.

Proceed to 2 and then to 3, if necessary. Do not look at anyone else other than your child. At this point, of course, parents wonder, "What are we going to do at 3? There's no rest-period room." This problem is easier to solve than you think.

BreakTime Room, BreakTime Place

Over the many years of developing the 1-2-3 Magic program, parents taught me what to do in situations like this. These were parents who, in the heat of battle, had to come up with rest-period solutions while in restaurants, theaters, stores, the museum, the ballpark, and church.

We call the solution "BreakTime Room, BreakTime Place." There is always a room, something like a room, or a symbolic place where a BreakTime can be served. For example, in the candy aisle conflict we just described, at the count of 3, some parents stay right where they are and hold the child's hand for several minutes. The adult says nothing during this period. That's a BreakTime room, BreakTime place. One young mother actually carried a small BreakTime mat around with her and would simply plop it onto the floor of the store when necessary.

Other parents have put little children in the grocery cart for the consequence. Other ideas include a corner of the store—a BreakTime place. For more rambunctious children, the bathroom of the store can serve the same purpose. Let them scream their heads off in there for a while. Some parents, feeling their children play up to an audience, will actually leave the grocery cart right where it is and take the child back to the car to do the rest period. Using the car like this makes some people ask, "Why should I have to go through all the trouble of leaving the store?"

The answer is because:

1. They're just kids.
2. They're still learning how to behave.
3. "All that trouble" is a sound investment in their future and your peace of mind.

Here's another idea. If the child is old enough and you won't worry about him, at the count of 3, have him wait for you—perhaps next to one of the cash registers or next to the information booth—until you're done shopping. Don't do this unless you're sure the child will be safe.

During any rest period, do not talk to the child. No lecturing, screaming, or nagging is allowed. Keeping quiet is often very hard, but after a while kids get the idea you mean business. And yes, there have been parents who felt the fuss was bad enough that they left a half-full grocery cart and went back home.

If the Kids Don't Want to Go

Imagine this situation: You're cooking a new recipe for dinner and you are so excited about this new dish that you can hardly stand it. At 5:15 p.m., however, you suddenly realize you are missing two essential ingredients. To make matters worse, your six-year-old and eight-year-old are in the other room playing well together for the first time in two and a half years. You're going to have to interrupt them, and there's no time to get a sitter.

> **Quik Tip**
>
> When you're out in public, there is always a room, something like a room, or a symbolic location where a BreakTime can be served. And don't forget your BreakTime alternatives. Just because people are watching does not mean that you have to be at your kids' mercy!

Here's what you do. Tell the kids that you have to go shopping. It will take about an hour, and they have to go with you. You know they don't want to, but you're stuck. Tell them the deal will be this: If they're "good" while you're out (meaning they don't hit a count of 4—you're giving them an extra count because of the length of the trip and because they don't want to go), you'll buy them a treat. Their reward will be a dollar in cash or a dollar's worth of whatever else they may want to buy. If they hit the count of 4 during the trip, however, the reward is gone.

Some parents feel this is bribery. It is! But the real definition of bribery is paying someone to do something illegal. Here we're paying the kids to do something legal, and it works.

If the Kids Do Want to Go

My wife and I had a very interesting experience using a BTA tactic with our kids when we initially tried going out for ice cream in the evening. The first few times we went out for our after-dinner treat, the kids fought like cats and dogs in the backseat. By the time we all got our ice cream, no one was in a party mood anymore.

So finally one evening I told the kids this: "Guys, we're going out for ice cream. But there's going to be a new deal. If you guys hit a count of 3 before we get to the store, we turn right around and come home. Nobody will get any ice cream."

With hopeful hearts, we took off in the car. The children started fighting. I said, "That's 1, and third count blows the trip." Sure enough, they were soon at 2, and then, only halfway to the ice cream store, they hit a 3. I turned the car around and went home. The BTA was the outing ending. The kids were not pleased; they looked stunned and resentful.

A few days later we took another shot at an ice cream outing. We weren't three hundred yards from the house when the kids started fighting again. I said, "That's 1, and third time blows the trip." They hit a 2 and then a 3, and the car got turned around and headed for home.

I'm sure that before our next attempt at an evening treat the kids had a conversation among themselves. It probably went something like this: "Isn't it a shame that most children in the world, except us, have normal fathers? Unfortunately, our dad turned out to be a shrink. But he's got the car and he's got the money, so if we want some ice cream, we'd better put up with his stupid games!"

So, about a week later, our intrepid group once again set out on its quest. To my amazement, the kids started fighting. As calmly as I could, I said, "That's 1, and third time blows the trip." To my further amazement the kids instantly became quiet, and they were good as gold the whole rest of the way. We all enjoyed our dessert.

The moral of this story: Sometimes it takes a few trials for you to make believers out of the kids. By the way, I've often been asked what to do if one child acts up on the way there and the other one doesn't. The answer: The one gets ice cream, and the other one doesn't. But don't expect to enjoy the ride home.

Keep Moving

Another tactic that some parents have used successfully in public takes us back to our grocery store example, where the child was having a major fit in the candy aisle. What some parents have done is simply leave the child on the floor and move on to the next aisle. They ask the next person they see, "Boy, do you hear all that racket over there?"

Seriously, what often happens is that the child starts worrying where Mom or Dad went, forgets the candy, and runs to find his parent. Naturally, you wouldn't want to get too far away, depending on the age of the child. Then again, some kids run to find their parent and then remember the candy and continue the tantrum. What should you do then?

The answer to this question depends on two things: How badly do you need to shop and how brave are you? A number of years ago, I was shopping by myself in our local grocery store. I saw a lady come in with a four-year-old boy. She picked the boy up, put him in a cart, and pushed the cart past the bubble-gum machine. The boy asked for gum, the mother said no, and the boy went ballistic. The mother kept moving and said nothing.

I shopped for twenty minutes, the mom shopped for twenty minutes, and the little boy howled for twenty minutes. Wherever you were in the store, which was not large, you could hear the kid's blood-curdling screams. But his mother was great. She paid no attention to her son. She had come in for milk, green pepper, and converted rice, and, by God, she was going out with milk, green pepper, and converted rice. I remember passing this duo in the rice aisle. While the child wailed, his mother was calmly looking at the rice box: "Let's see, four ounces times six. Yes, that should be enough for tonight."

I was impressed. But Mom was soon to fall off her pedestal. I hurried along because I wanted to get out of the noisy store. I got to the checkout line. The racket behind me started getting louder. There they were. This lady and her unhappy son got in the next line, and she checked out sooner than I did because she had fewer items. With great relief I watched her leaving the store, with her son still yelling. As she passed the bubble-gum machine for the second time, she stopped and bought her son a piece of gum!

I was dumbfounded. I almost lost all my professional decorum right there. I wanted to jump over the counter, run up to this woman, and say, "Excuse me, ma'am. You don't know me, but I'm a clinical psychologist. Could I talk to you for a moment?" This mother had just rewarded a twenty-minute tantrum.

> **Caution**
> Never reward tantrums by giving the child what he or she wants! You're only guaranteeing more tantrums in the future.

There may be times out in public when, in spite of everything you've done, your child won't stop a tantrum. Your choices then are these: gut it out and finish your shopping while the child continues his tantrum, take the child out to the car until he stops screaming, or go home.

Don't Take Them Unless You Have To

Have you ever been to church on Sunday, and in the row ahead of you is a couple with a two-year-old? The two-year-old, of course, isn't paying any attention to the service. Neither are his parents, since they are preoccupied with trying to keep their son in line so he won't bother other people. Finally, sitting around this family trio are ten other individuals who aren't paying any attention to the service either, because they're busy evaluating how well the couple is disciplining their two-year-old. While "cry rooms," where parents with young kids can go to avoid bothering others during worship services, are common in many churches today, they aren't always available.

So, in the absence of a cry room, we have thirteen people who might as well not have gone to church at all. Of course, we're not trying to talk you out of going to church, but think before you go anywhere. Don't ask for unnecessary trouble in public by putting your kids in situations they simply can't handle. In our church example, while the parents are trying their hardest not to allow their son to bother the other people around them, these other people are being distracted anyway.

Tips for Riding in the Car

Traveling in the car is a kind of half-public, half-private experience that can present parents with some extremely difficult and even dangerous situations. Parents often feel like

> **Quik Tip**
> Traveling in the car with the kids can be aggravating, and that can also make driving dangerous. Parents often feel like an unwilling but captive audience to their kids' misbehavior in the car. Never fear! You have a number of tactics available to you.

an unwilling captive audience to their children's misbehavior in the car. And making matters worse, moms and dads know their discipline options are limited when they're behind the wheel.

Have you ever driven on an interstate with your left hand on the steering wheel while your right hand is waving madly through the backseat, trying to grab the kid who's just been teasing his sister for the fifty-seventh time since you left the last town? Vacations are supposed to be fun, but this kind of routine is not fun. I've had many parents tell me that they pretty much stopped taking vacations because of nasty and repeated scenes like these.

Counting is very useful while chauffeuring the kids around town. The question, of course, is what to do at 3. BreakTime alternatives are one choice. One couple, for example, didn't allow anyone to talk—including Mom and Dad—for fifteen minutes after the kids hit 3 for behavior like teasing, fighting, or badgering. Other families have used fines (money taken off the allowance) at the rate of so many cents for each minute that would have been included in the child's normal BreakTime.

But being in the car doesn't prevent you from doing a good, old-fashioned rest period. Where is the BreakTime room? You're riding in it! Your car is actually a stylish, gas-guzzling BreakTime room. Over the years a very effective tactic for many of my parents has been to count 1-2-3, then pull the car to the side of the road for the rest period. This strategy is dramatic and has quite an impact on the children. Parents can either sit quietly in the car with their children while they're serving the rest period, or get out and take the opportunity to stretch their legs a bit.

For some reason, counting the kids in the car and having them serve the BreakTimes when they get home doesn't work as well, unless you're very close to home. The problem may be that the rest period comes too long after the offense. In addition, the demand for a rest period when you walk in the door may simply start another fight, because often by the time you get home everybody has forgotten the original problem.

On longer car rides and on vacations, counting can be used as effectively as on short trips. But other tactics are often helpful.

Some alternative tactics that parents have used successfully in the car include the usual—and very helpful—activities like the alphabet game and car bingo. Putting one child in the front seat and one in the back can help, as can using a DVD player (and renting twenty movies!) or leaving at four in the morning so the kids sleep away the largest part of a four- or five-hour ride. Telling the kids they get fifty cents for every goat they see is also a brilliant maneuver to keep their attention focused on something other than torturing each other.

The main point is this: don't ever leave on a car ride with the kids—especially on a long "vacation"—without putting on your thinking cap first. Have the 1-2-3 and a few other tactics in your hip pocket, because you're going to need them.

Two Stressed-Out Brains?

Being out in public can mean more stress for a child's brain and also more stress for your adult brain. There is additional and novel sensory information for your child to process, requiring more brain energy, which can be fatiguing. There are new sights, sounds, smells, and people to understand. In addition, there is often less structure when you're out and about, and with less structure comes more unknown. What should your child expect, and what is expected of your child?

Your adult brain must also work harder. What should you require of your child in public? What if your child acts up in front of a host of witnesses? The key for you is remaining calm and decisive by knowing exactly what you'll do if a discipline problem pops up suddenly. Also, key to your child's brain welfare is that the two of you have a good time together!

Now that you understand something about counting (as well as what to do when your child misbehaves in public), let's take a look at our 1-2-3 Magic **Real-Life Story 1**. *The Case of the Temper Tantrum Terrorist* will explain in detail how one couple implemented counting with their five-year-old son.

Real-Life Story 1

COUNTING OBNOXIOUS BEHAVIOR

When they are starting the 1-2-3 Magic program, most parents begin by simply counting obnoxious behavior for a few days to a week before they do anything with Parenting Jobs 2 and 3—encouraging good behavior and strengthening relationships. That's the way my husband and I handled it, and it was a good move!

In *The Case of the Temper Tantrum Terrorist*, you'll meet our young five-year-old son, Zach. Before we started 1-2-3 Magic, this kid was a handful. While I've heard that many children (about 50 percent) will shape up in just a few days with counting, it took us about a week to make Zach a believer.

Here's our story. In the **Before** section, you'll see two bewildered parents trying to discipline their child without a concrete plan. Then you'll sit in on our process of **Thinking It Through** before we get around to handling our son the right way in the **After** section.

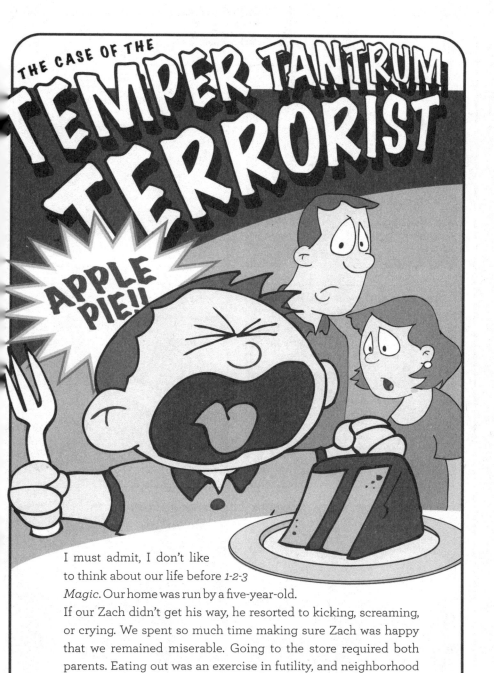

I must admit, I don't like to think about our life before *1-2-3 Magic*. Our home was run by a five-year-old. If our Zach didn't get his way, he resorted to kicking, screaming, or crying. We spent so much time making sure Zach was happy that we remained miserable. Going to the store required both parents. Eating out was an exercise in futility, and neighborhood barbecues were politely declined because we couldn't count on Zach to behave himself at someone else's house.

One night we took a chance and went to a local restaurant...

BEFORE

BEFORE

Not our proudest moments as parents.

Well, the first round went to Zach—in a sense. Actually, it didn't go to anybody, since we all wound up feeling miserable. You can't beat public humiliation for pure fun—and, believe me, we'd been through plenty of scenes like the one you just witnessed.

We just couldn't keep on like this. We were getting discouraged, and we had to do something different. But exactly what was that "something" going to be?

Feeling desperate, I decided to try a product that I thought at the time would be a long shot.

THINKING IT THROUGH

THINKING IT THROUGH

After our talk, there were times when I thought my husband understood what I was saying, but most of the time I felt I wasn't getting anywhere. He hadn't read the book, so I got the *1-2-3 Magic* DVD (which I thought was just as good as the book). My husband hinted—but only hinted—that he might be willing to watch the DVD, but only if I wasn't in the room!

Why are adult males so hard to talk to? Zach's behavior remained awful. As far as I was concerned, we were still in a big pickle—stuck with nowhere to go.

Then one day a miracle occurred.

THINKING IT THROUGH

My husband actually watched the *1-2-3 Magic* DVD. And he liked it!

We practiced counting on each other.

THAT'S 2.

We whispered about our plans—Zach's suspicious eyes watched us.

I CAN BEAT THIS.

We had the Kickoff Conversation.

ZACH, WE'RE GOING TO DO SOME THINGS DIFFERENT AROUND HERE.

My husband and I were a team! We were ready for whatever Zach could throw at us.

AFTER

AFTER

Once he calmed down, five minutes was counted. He came out with puffy eyes and ate his chicken and rice.

We were elated! The 1-2-3 worked! It would be easy sailing from here on out.

Not so fast. Right after dinner this scene took place.

AFTER

He was picked up and carried to his room. He screamed again.

Once in his room he laid on the floor. He was quiet! And then he took his bath!!

When my husband and I went to bed, we were so excited. We did it!

But the next day was worse. And the day after was even worse than that.
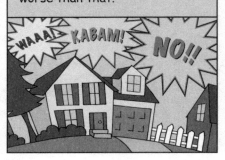

Zach spent 50% of his time in time-out.

AFTER

Since our "week from hell," things have been very different around our house. Our son now knows that when we say something, we mean business. No yelling, no empty threats. Sure, he still pushes the limits at times, but he doesn't get anywhere.

We've also advanced our use of *1-2-3 Magic* to the strategies for encouraging good behavior (like getting Zach to bed) and to doing things that reinforce the bond between us (like shared fun). Since we have learned how to control Zach's oppositional moments, it is so much easier to like him!

The last thing we would have wanted to hear when beginning *1-2-3 Magic* was that we would have to go through a hell week before seeing results. But we also would never have believed stories about a child shaping up in just a few hours, even though we've heard it has happened many times!

We hope our harrowing tale has given you some encouragement!

Now let's go back to explaining the basics of 1-2-3 Magic.

8

HOW TO HANDLE SIBLING RIVALRY, TANTRUMS, POUTING, AND LYING

Managing Four Common Behavioral Problems

FOUR COMMON, BUT AGGRAVATING Stop behaviors require a few modifications in our basic procedures. Sibling rivalry, tantrums, pouting, and lying are issues that many parents put near the top of their list of horribly aggravating and repetitive behaviors. Here's what to do.

Sibling Rivalry

Your life gets exponentially more complicated when you have more than one child acting up. Now there are multiple actors in the drama. How are you going to handle the situation? Sibling rivalry will never go away completely, but here are a few simple rules to follow:

> **Guideline 1: Count both kids.** When the children are fighting, you should count both kids most of the time, unless one is the obvious, unprovoked aggressor. Usually they both helped produce the conflict. Be careful—kids are tricky! Some provoke in subtle ways and others in more overt ways, so it is often hard to tell who started a fight—even if you are right there watching.

> **Caution**
> Never ask the world's two most ridiculous questions, "Who started it?" and "What happened?" unless you think someone is physically injured. Do you expect your kids to come up with George Washington's version of "I cannot tell a lie"?

For example, maybe you're driving the car with the kids in the back and you hear, "Mom, he's looking at me again!" Who started that one? There's really no way to tell. In that case, you should count both children.

> **Guideline 2: Never ask the world's two most ridiculous questions.** Every parent knows what these questions are: "What happened?" and "Who started it?" What do you expect to hear, a version of George Washington's "I cannot tell a lie"? "Yes, I started this fight, and the last thirteen consecutive squabbles have also been my personal responsibility." That kind of confession won't happen. Instead, all you get is the kids blaming each another and yelling.

There are, of course, times when you might need to ask what happened. If, for instance, you think someone might be physically injured, you should examine the child and find out what caused the injury. The same thing might be true with other serious or unusual cases. But for your run-of-the-mill instances of sibling rivalry, trying to find out what happened is too often a lost cause.

> **Guideline 3: Don't expect an older child to act more mature during a fight than a younger child.** Even if your two kids are eleven years old and four years old, don't say to the

eleven-year-old, "She's only a baby. Can't you put up with a little teasing?" That comment is the equivalent of loading the gun of the four-year-old, who will be sure to both appreciate your generosity in providing ammo and take maximum advantage of it.

Along these same lines, imagine for a second that your eleven-year-old son comes up to you one day and says, "I want to ask you a question."

"Go ahead," you say.

"How come I always get a ten-minute rest period, and Miss Shrimp over there (your four-year-old) only has to go for five minutes?"

"Because the rule in our house," you say, "is one minute of BreakTime for each year of your life."

"WELL, THAT'S THE DUMBEST THING I EVER HEARD OF!"

"That's 1."

This child doesn't really want information; he wants a fight. Don't get sidetracked with a useless argument, and remember that you should always start counting when your child attacks and save your energy for true discussions.

Sharing Spaces

What if the kids have a fight and they share the same room? It would not be a good idea to send two fighting children to the same place to continue their fight. Send one to his room and the other to an alternate room or place. Then for the next rest period reverse the locations. Or use BreakTime alternatives when both children fight. If your kids have separate bedrooms and they fight on the way to their rest periods, extend the BreakTimes by five or ten minutes.

Temper Tantrums

Tantrums can be counted or ignored. You might choose to ignore your two-year-old thrashing around on the living room floor after you refused to give him your entire milk shake. You can even leave the room if you think the child will be safe. But you might want to count your ten-year-old's verbal abuse after you wouldn't let him have a friend over.

In either case, there is a basic rule about dealing with fits of temper: never talk or argue with a tantruming child. That's the same as pouring gasoline on a fire. Counting is OK because it's a signal rather than a conversation.

So let's say you chose BreakTime for your six-year-old son for tantruming. He's now in his room and he's still having a fit. What if the rest period is up but the child's not done with the tantrum? You don't want to let him out in his condition, and in a sense, he's just earned another rest period. Fortunately, the answer to this dilemma is simple. If the child is four or older, the BreakTime doesn't start until the tantrum is over. So if it takes him fifteen minutes to calm down, the rest period starts after fifteen minutes. And if it takes the kid two hours to calm down (he could be a room wrecker!), the BreakTime starts after two hours.

Resist the temptation to stick your head into his room every five or ten minutes saying things like, "Come on now, don't you think that's enough? We miss you. Dinner's in five minutes and you have homework to do." Just leave him alone until he's tired of being angry.

The only children we don't use this temper-tantrum modification for are the two- and three-year-olds. They don't seem to get the idea, so just let them out after a couple of minutes, even if they're still tantruming, and cross your fingers. Once they're out, ignoring the child is usually more effective than trying to talk him out of his irritation. If he still doesn't quiet down, leave him in a little longer the next time.

One caution. Some kids will tantrum due to sensory issues. Their socks or shoes or sweater literally rubs them the wrong way. These sensory irritabilities are not misbehavior, nor does the child choose to be this way. Take the child's opinions seriously, and avoid the offending smells, tastes, or feels.

Pouting

Pouting is a passive behavior that is designed to make you feel guilty. Try not to feel guilty when your child sulks after receiving consequences for misbehavior. Why should you feel bad for trying to be a good parent? Remember: the demanding, firm part of parenting is essential to the job, even if it temporarily upsets your child.

So if you discipline a child and she gives you the ultimate in martyr looks, just turn around, say nothing, and walk away. The only time you would do something different is if you get what we call an "aggressive pouter." An aggressive pouter is a child who follows you all over the house to make sure you don't miss a minute of her sour face. If she does, "That's 1." She's trying to rub your nose in her grumpiness, and you're not going to allow her to do that.

Lying

Counting is not always useful for lying, for two reasons. One reason is lying is a more serious offense that should be addressed immediately, and the second reason is lying is often used to cover up other misbehaviors. Lying drives some parents crazy, and managing this problem is often confusing and difficult, so we'll try to provide some basic guidelines to help you deal with it.

There are basically two kinds of lies. The first kind involves making up stories that are designed to impress other people and build up one's ego. This type of verbal fabrication is not common in children, who don't feel the same kind of pressure to influence others' opinions of them that adults do. The second—and by far the most common type—is lying to avoid trouble. These lies may involve covering up a past misdeed or trying to get out of some unpleasant task. Kids who steal, for example, will almost always lie about the theft when they are initially confronted. Other kids lie about not having homework so they won't have to face that boring job.

In dealing with lying, parents should first remember not to

overreact. Not telling the truth certainly isn't a good thing, but it's not usually a truly terrible behavior. Many parents get so upset about lying that they act as though the world is coming to an end. These upset grown-ups accomplish two things: (1) they lead the child to believe that he is a horrible person, and (2) they increase the probability of more lies in the future. That's because kids who are afraid that you'll get upset have a very strong tendency to take the easy way out first when you confront them. That means lying! They want to escape the hot seat—right now.

What Should You Do about Lying?

Imagine that the school calls on Tuesday at 1:00 p.m. to tell you that your ten-year-old son, Tom, got into a fight with a boy named Davey Smith at lunchtime. At three forty-five Tom comes home. Mom starts the conversation like this:
"How was your day?"
"Good. You made me my favorite sandwich for lunch."
"Speaking of lunchtime, how did that go?"
"Fine, we played some baseball."
"Anything unusual happen?"
"No."
"OK, listen, young man. You're lying to me. I got a call from the school today, and Mr. Pasquini told me you got into a fight with..." and so on.

In this conversation the parent is "cornering" her son. Sure, Mom wants to get some information from Tom, but first she wants to test him to see if he'll tell her the truth. This is not the best way to handle the situation.

When you know some kind of trouble has occurred, don't corner children or trick them into telling you something you know is not true. Imagine that one night right after dinner you give your child the third degree about whether or not he has homework. He denies having any homework six times and then finally, after your seventh question, he breaks down and admits that he has some math to do. By this time you are furious, but you also feel victorious that you finally got the truth out of the kid.

But what has really just happened? You have given your child six times to practice lying! You may think to yourself, "Sooner or later he'll realize he can't fool me and he'll give up." Sometimes kids will give up, but many children will continue trying to take the easy way out first. They will simply work to become better liars, and you will be providing them with their practice sessions.

Here's a more constructive approach. Imagine that your child has misbehaved in some way. If you don't know the truth about what occurred, ask the child once what happened. If he tells you the story and you find out later that he lied, punish him for whatever the offense was as well as for the lie.

Try not to surprise the child by asking your question on the spur of the moment. Many kids simply respond impulsively. They lie, but their real desire is just to end the conversation, get rid of you, and stay out of trouble.

What if something bad has happened and you already know all the gory details? You might say something like this: "I want you to tell me the story of what happened at lunch today, but not right now. Think about it a while and we'll talk in fifteen minutes. But remember I already talked with Mr. Pasquini." No lectures or tantrums from you.

Many parents use another option when (1) they already know what happened and (2) the child is very likely to lie about the event no matter how the questions are phrased. In this case you simply tell the child what you know and then calmly mete out the punishment. You do not even give the child the chance to lie. Under these circumstances many kids will blow up and accuse you of not trusting them. Manage their reaction by ignoring their statement or counting them, and end the conversation with, "I'm sure you'll do better next time."

When you have a child who uses lying regularly to avoid unpleasant tasks, such as chores or homework, try to fix the problem—as much as you can—so that lying does not seem necessary to the child.

If your son continually lies about homework, for example, work out some kind of communication with the teacher, such as a daily assignment sheet. Then use the tactics described in chapter 16, such as the PNP routine and Rough Checkout to ensure that the homework is being completed. For chores, consider fixing the problem by the judicious use of other Start behavior strategies (see chapter 12).

Lying is not a good thing and you don't want to encourage it in your children, but it certainly isn't the end of the world either. Most people, children as well as adults, probably tell a few "stretchers" from time to time. Not telling the truth doesn't mean that your kids don't love you or that they are bound to grow up to become inmates in a federal penitentiary. Lying can turn into a significant problem, though, and it needs to be managed carefully and thoughtfully. Over the years, frequent emotional overreactions from you—combined with badgering and cornering—can help produce an accomplished liar.

Now let's take a look at **Real-Life Story 2**. In *The Incredible Case of the Traveling Troublemakers*, you'll see how one young mom used counting very effectively to deal with her squabbling offspring while riding in the car!

Real-Life Story 2

SIBLING RIVALRY

Parenting is a difficult and complicated job. Admit it—it's a lot harder than you imagined it would be before you had kids! Once our little ones showed up in our house, there they were—period. No escape and no going out without getting a babysitter.

Before we had children, my husband and I imagined the warm, fuzzy, peaceful, and affectionate times we would have with our family—and we did get to enjoy plenty of those moments. But after several years of parenting experience, we quickly learned that we also had to manage whining, teasing, tantrums, messiness, and stubbornness.

And we found out that managing two kids is a lot harder than one. Sibling rivalry is chronic, and it's one of the most aggravating things parents have to deal with. Managing and minimizing kids' fighting is part of Parenting Job 1.

Check out our story...

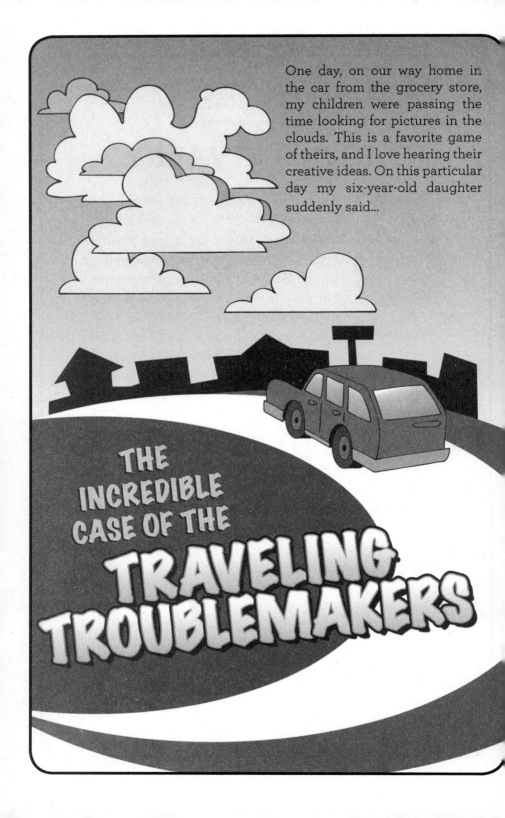

One day, on our way home in the car from the grocery store, my children were passing the time looking for pictures in the clouds. This is a favorite game of theirs, and I love hearing their creative ideas. On this particular day my six-year-old daughter suddenly said...

THE INCREDIBLE CASE OF THE TRAVELING TROUBLEMAKERS

You guessed it. It was a police officer!

He came walking up to my door.

"IS EVERYTHING OK, MA'AM?"

I explained my children were fighting, so I pulled over and we were taking a time-out.

"THAT'S A GOOD IDEA AND A SAFE ONE! HAVE A GOOD DAY."

He smiled, then just looked at the kids and waved to them. They seemed to be in shock!

It was silent the rest of the way home. They have not even attempted fighting in the car again—yet!

Sibling Rivalry: Eternal, Evolutionary, Aggravating!

It may surprise you to learn that sibling rivalry is actually good for your kids' brains! Your kids' brains are learning how to create and maintain intimate relationships—a tough job. They are rewiring their brains for social connection and emotional stability, and there is a lot of fighting that happens along the way. As parents, our job is to teach children to control their emotions and behaviors through communication. When you count your children, you discourage fighting and encourage other methods of conflict resolution.

Sibling rivalry is a sign of normal, instinctive childhood competition. It is not a sign of bad parenting!

CHAPTER SUMMARY

Sibling rivalry, tantrums, pouting, and lying present unique behavior management problems for parents. That's why we put them in a separate chapter. When these issues arise, put on your thinking cap and take a deep breath. Then you should be ready for anything!

9
GETTING STARTED WITH COUNTING

How to Talk to Your Kids about 1-2-3 Magic and the New House Rules

A QUESTION PEOPLE OFTEN ask at seminars is, "Do you explain to the kids what you're going to be doing?" The answer is yes. Starting the 1-2-3 program is fairly easy. The Kickoff Conversation only takes about five minutes, and a little rehearsing beforehand only takes a few minutes more. But don't put a lot of stock in the impact of this initial conversation. Wishful thinking on your part will not do the job. Lots of children don't really get the idea until they've been counted for a while and been to their rooms a few times, or until after they've seen their siblings counted.

If both parents are living at home, or even if Mom and Dad live in separate places, it's preferable if both grown-ups sit down together with the children and do the initial explaining. If you have an ex and you don't get along, do the Kickoff separately or the tension between you and your former partner could interfere with the explanation.

Getting Started

Here's one way to start: "Listen, you guys know there are times when you do things we don't care for, like arguing, whining, and teasing. From now on we're going to do something different. When we see you doing something you're not supposed to do, we'll say, 'That's 1.' That's a warning, and it means you're supposed to stop. If you don't stop, we'll say, 'That's 2.' That will be your second warning. If you still don't stop, we'll say, 'That's 3. Take five (or however many minutes equals your age).' That means you have to go to your room for a break. It's like a kind of rest period. When you come out, we don't talk about what happened unless it's really necessary. We just forget it and start over."

"By the way, kids, there's part of this new system that you'll like and part you won't like. Here's what you won't like: if the thing you do is bad enough to start with, like swearing or hitting, we'll say, 'That's 3. Take ten or fifteen.' That means there aren't any other warnings. You just go straight to your room, and the time will be longer.

"The part you will like is that most of the time we won't talk about what happened after a rest period. Well, that's the new deal. It's pretty simple. Do you have any questions?"

You can expect the kids to sit there and look at you like you've just gone off your rocker. Some kids will poke each other and exchange knowing glances, as if to say, "Well, it looks like Mom went to the library again and got another one of those books on how to raise us. Last time she stuck to it for about four days, and Dad never did anything different at all. I think if we stick together and hang tough, we should be running the house again inside of a week, right?"

Don't expect your kids to be grateful, to look enlightened, or to

> **Quik Tip**
> It's very important to rehearse or role-play the counting procedure for older children as well as little kids. This gives the children a real feel for what's going to happen when you start counting, and it also lets them know you're serious about addressing their behavior in a new way.

thank you for your efforts to raise them responsibly. Just get going, stick to your guns, and—when in doubt—count!

Dress Rehearsal

Now you can have some fun. Since some two-, three-, and four-year-olds won't understand everything you've just said, it's a good idea to rehearse or role-play counting for them. It's also very important to rehearse with the older children. Rehearsing the procedure gives the kids a feel for what's going to happen and also tells the children you're serious.

Here's what you say next: "Kids, let's practice counting. Who wants to start? OK, Kieran, pretend you're whining at me for candy. Can you do a good whine?" (Kid whines). "Wow, that was a good whine! Now I'll say, 'That's 1.' Now whine again…" And so on.

Now take them through the rest of the procedure, so they get a feel for being counted, hitting three, getting to the BreakTime room or chair, serving the time, and then being let out. Make sure you praise them in an age-appropriate way for their cooperation.

Other possible role plays: The little ones can count a stuffed animal. Mom and Dad can count each other (after one pretends to be a misbehaving kid). The kids can count you, and you go to time-out. While on your way to your break, don't go like a Goody Two-Shoes. Grumble a little! The message: it's OK to not like being counted and going to BreakTime.

Once you start counting, and once the kids know you're serious, many children will respond well quickly. Some kids will shape up within the first few hours; some, within the first few days. Little toddlers may take a week or so to get the idea. Remain gentle and persistent, and keep your talking to a minimum.

At this point, you may feel that you're ready to start using the 1-2-3 program. But remember—about half of kids will struggle with the counting system and continue to act out despite being counted. In the next chapter, we'll discuss the Six Kinds of Testing and Manipulation that your kids might use to derail the 1-2-3 Magic program, and how you can prepare for those behaviors to keep your family on track.

The Brain Seeks Organization and Control

Adult brains perform best when they *anticipate* what's going to happen, *categorize* new information, and *control* responses when things do happen. So do children's brains. The Kickoff Conversation will help you and your children prepare for and rehearse *1-2-3 Magic*.

Having a plan for responding well to your children's behavior helps you perform at an optimal level. It allows you to be able to respond with little emotion and little talking. You can quickly anticipate your child's response, categorize it as a start or stop behavior, and control your reaction. This model then teaches your child to do the same thing!

CHAPTER SUMMARY

You're almost ready to begin your first giant parenting step:

Controlling Obnoxious Behavior!

PART III

Managing Testing and Manipulation

CHAPTER 10
Recognizing the Six Types of Testing and Manipulation

CHAPTER 11
Tales from the Trenches

10
RECOGNIZING THE SIX TYPES OF TESTING AND MANIPULATION

How to Prepare for Kids Resisting 1-2-3 Magic

WHEN YOU ARE IN the warm, friendly parenting mode, you will usually not be frustrating your children. When you are operating from the demanding, firm side, however, you will be! As a parent, you have to regularly frustrate your children in three main ways: (1) ask them to start doing things they don't want to do (homework, going to bed), (2) ask them to stop doing things they do want to do (teasing, whining), and (3) not give them something they want (cookie, toy).

When you are frustrating your little ones, the children have two choices. First, they can cooperate with what you want and tolerate their own frustration. Most kids gradually learn that frustration is not the end of the world, and as they mature they begin to get a sense that putting up with present aggravations may actually be the route to future rewards. That ability to delay gratification now for something better later is one foundation of emotional intelligence.

On the other hand, frustrated children can engage in what we call testing and manipulation. These are the efforts of the less-powerful child to get what he wants or to avoid discipline by making his parent emotionally confused and consequently sidetracked.

Three Things to Remember about Testing and Manipulation

1. **Testing occurs when a child is frustrated.** You are not giving him the potato chips he wants; you are counting him; you are making him do homework or go to bed. He doesn't like this and hopes for a way to get what he wants in spite of the obstacle (you).
2. **Testing, therefore, is purposeful behavior.** The primary purpose of a child's testing, obviously, is to get his way rather than have you impose your will on him. If the child still doesn't get his way, testing and manipulation can have a secondary purpose: *revenge*.
3. **When engaging in testing and manipulation, a child has a choice of six basic tactics.** All six can serve the primary purpose of getting one's way, and five of the six tactics can serve the secondary purpose of revenge. Often a child's testing behavior will represent a combination of one or more of the six basic tactics.

All parents will recognize the manipulative tactics we are about to describe; you have likely encountered each of them many times with your children. Grown-ups are usually aware—if they think about it—of which maneuvers are used by which children. Moms and dads may also recognize some of their own favorite strategies,

Key Concept
The first goal of testing is for the child to get what he wants. Since he's less powerful than you are, he must use emotional manipulation. If the child still fails to get what he wants, the second goal of testing is often retaliation or revenge. The kid is going to make you pay for not letting him get his way!

since adults use the same basic manipulative methods to get what they want.

By the way, the use of testing and manipulation does not mean that a child is emotionally troubled or in need of psychological care. Attempts to get your way, as well as attempts to punish the bigger people who don't give you your way, are perfectly normal human psychological tactics. The use of testing also does not require an exceptionally high IQ. In fact, adults are often amazed at how naturally and skillfully little kids can produce and modify complex testing strategies. Because our sons and daughters are so naturally skilled, it is very important that adult caregivers understand children's testing tactics and how to manage them.

The Six Basic Testing Tactics

Here are the six fundamental strategies that children use to try to influence the adults who are frustrating them.

1. Badgering: "Why? Why? Why? Why?"

Badgering is the "Please, please, please, please!" or "Why, why, why?" routine. "Just this once! Just this once! Just this once! Just this once!" "Mom! Mom! Mom! Mom! Mom!" Some children could have been machine guns during the last war. The child keeps after you and after you and after you, trying to wear you down with repetition. "Just give me what I want and I'll shut up!" is the underlying message.

Badgering can be particularly taxing when it is done loudly and in public. Some parents attempt to respond to everything the frustrated child says every time she says it. Mom or Dad may try to explain, to reassure, or to distract the child. As badgering continues, parents can become more and more desperate, going on the equivalent of a verbal wild-goose chase—searching for the right words or reasons to make the child keep quiet. However, many kids are extremely single-minded once their badgering starts. They won't stop until either they get what they want or their parent uses a more effective approach to stop the testing.

Badgering is what we refer to as a great "blender" tactic, since it mixes easily with other manipulative strategies. The basic element in badgering, of course, is repetition. So when any of the other verbal testing tactics are repeated again and again, the resulting manipulative strategy is a combination of that other tactic plus the repetitive power of badgering.

2. Temper (Intimidation): "I HATE YOU!"

Displays of temper, or what we sometimes refer to as intimidation, involve obvious, aggressive behavior. Younger children whose language skills aren't quite as developed may throw themselves on the floor, bang their heads, holler at the top of their lungs, and kick around ferociously. Older kids may come up with arguments that accuse you of being unjust, illogical, or simply a bad parent in general. When frustrated, older kids may also swear or complain angrily.

Some children's fits of temper go on for very long periods. Many ADHD and bipolar children, for example, have been known to rant and rave for more than an hour at a time. In the process they may damage property or trash their rooms. Tantrums will be prolonged even further if (1) the child has an audience; (2) the adults involved continue talking, arguing, or pleading with the child; or (3) the adults don't know how to handle the aggression.

Temper fits in two-year-olds can be aggravating, but they can also be funny. My wife took a picture of our son when he was an energetic toddler having a temper tantrum right in the middle of the ashes in the fireplace at my parents' home. (The fire was not going, of course.) We all can still laugh at that scene.

As kids get older and more powerful, tantrums get more worrisome and just plain scarier. That's why we like to see them well controlled or eliminated by the time a child is five or six.

3. Threat: "I'm going to run away from home!"

Frustrated kids often threaten their parents with dire predictions if the adults don't come across with the desired goods. Here are a few examples:

"I'm going to run away from home!"
"I'll never speak to you again!"
"I'm going to kill myself!"
"I'm not eating dinner and I won't do my homework!"

The message is clear: something bad is going to happen unless you give me what I want immediately. Give me the Twinkie right before dinner, stop counting me, don't make me go to bed, *or else*! Some of the threats that younger children come up with are funny. One little girl, whose mother was trying to get her to go to bed, angrily shouted, "All right, I'll go. But I'm going to lie there all night with my eyes open!"

Another child, a six-year-old boy, was counted and timed out by his father for squirting the dog with a hose. The boy threatened to run away, actually packed a small bag, and walked out the front door. After five minutes, however, he walked back in the door and yelled at his dad, "I couldn't run away because you guys won't let me cross the street!"

Other threats are not funny. Some frustrated children threaten to kill themselves, and this is something no parent takes lightly. Parents wonder if these threats are just manipulative or if their child really wants to die. Two questions can help parents sort out this dilemma. First of all, is this child generally happy? Does she enjoy life most of the time, have friends, do OK in school, and fit into the family? If the answers to these questions are positive, it is less likely that the child truly wants to end her life. Second, did the suicidal threat come out of the blue or was the comment a response to some obvious recent frustration? If "I'm going to kill myself" comes out of nowhere, the threat is always more worrisome and needs to be looked into.

4. Martyrdom: "I never get anything!"

Martyr-like testing tactics are a perennial favorite of children. When using martyrdom, the child may indicate that his life has become totally unfair and an incredible burden. "No one around here loves me anymore," "I never get anything," or "You like her more than me" are examples.

Or the child may actually do something that has a self-punitive, self-denying flavor, such as not eating dinner, sitting in the closet for an hour, or staring out the window without talking. Crying, pouting, and simply looking sad or teary can also be useful manipulative devices.

The goal of martyrdom, obviously, is to make the parent feel guilty, and martyrdom can be surprisingly effective. This testing tactic is very difficult for adults to handle. Many moms and dads seem to have a guilt button the size of the state of Wyoming! All the kids have to do is push that button and they wind up running the house.

Children learn early on that parents are highly invested in the welfare of their offspring. Kids know their caregivers want them to be safe, happy, and healthy. Unfortunately, kids also seem to naturally appreciate the logical consequence of this adult commitment. Acting hurt or deprived can be a powerful way of influencing adult behavior.

Two-year-olds, for example, will sometimes hold their breath until they turn blue when they are mad about not getting what they want. Many parents wonder how a child could even come up with an idea like that. One creative child, whose mother had just sent her to her bedroom, was heard yelling out her window, "I can't breathe! I can't breathe!" This tactic may have been creative, but it was not effective.

5. Butter Up: "You're the nicest dad in the world!"

The fifth tactic, butter up, takes an approach that's different from the first four. Instead of making you feel uncomfortable, the child tries to make you feel good. You may run the risk of losing this good feeling if you subsequently frustrate the child.

"Gee, Mom, you've got the prettiest eyes of anybody on the

block" is a fairly blatant example. Or, "I think I'll go clean my room. It's been looking kind of messy for the last three weeks. And after that maybe I'll take a look at the garage."

With butter up, the basic message from child to parent is: "You'll feel really bad if you mistreat or discipline or deny me after how nice I've been to you." Butter up is intended to be an advance setup for parental guilt. The child is implying, "You'll feel so positively toward me that you won't have the heart to make me feel bad."

Children can use promises as butter-up manipulation. "Please, Mom. Please. I'll eat my dinner and I promise I won't even ask for any dessert," said one little girl who wanted a snack at five in the afternoon. Some promises kids make are impossibilities. One little boy, while in the process of pressing his father for a new computer, said, "I'll never ask you for anything ever again."

Apologies can be sincere, but they can also be examples of butter-up testing. "I'm sorry, I'm sorry. I said I'm sorry," one little boy pleaded in an attempt to avoid being grounded for socking his little brother.

Butter-up manipulation is obviously the least obnoxious of all the testing tactics. In fact, some people don't think it should be labeled as testing at all. It is true that butter up is sometimes hard to distinguish from genuine affection. If a child says "I love you" and doesn't ask for anything immediately afterward, it's probably genuine affection. And a child who asks if he can have a friend over if he cleans up his room may be proposing a straightforward and legitimate deal. But if you've ever heard a parent say, "The only time my son's ever nice is when he wants something," that person is probably referring to the butter-up tactic.

6. Physical Tactics: Pow! Whack! Bam!

From a parent's perspective, this form of testing is perhaps the worst strategy of all. Here the frustrated child may physically attack an adult, break something, or run away. Physical methods of trying to get one's way are more common in smaller children who don't have well-developed language skills. When the use of this type of testing continues beyond age four or five, we begin to worry. Some kids have a long history of this kind of behavior, and the bigger the child gets, the scarier their use of physical strategies gets.

For example, some parents who use BreakTimes tell us that their children sometimes physically attack when the parent is trying to escort the child to the BreakTime area. Some children become quite ferocious—kicking, biting, scratching, pinching, and hitting while yelling at the top of their lungs.

Other frustrated, physically oriented kids will smash or break things—sometimes even their own possessions. One ten-year-old boy, for instance, was sent to his room for fighting with his brother. The door to his bedroom happened to be shut when he got to it, so he gave it one of his best karate kicks, cracking the door down the middle. Another boy smashed a coffee mug on the tile floor in the front hall of the house. Unfortunately, one of the larger pieces of the mug went flying into the glass storm door, which shattered.

Another physical testing tactic, running away, is not used a lot by younger children. Threats to run away appear more often in kids under seven. One seven-year-old boy used a different version of this idea on his mother, who had just denied his request to go outside. The boy sneaked down to the basement and hid for two hours, not responding to anyone who called his name. The tactic was effective, at least in punishing his mother, who was beside herself with worry.

What's Going On Here?

Most kids, of course, would never be able to describe the underlying mechanics of testing. But we can tell you exactly what's going on. Here's how it works: The six testing and manipulation tactics share a common dynamic. Without quite knowing what he's doing, the child is in effect saying to the parent: "Look, you're making me uncomfortable by not giving me what I want. You're making me get out of bed, you're counting me for teasing my sister, or you're not buying me a treat. But now I'm also making you uncomfortable with my badgering, tantrums, ominous statements, etc. Now that we're both uncomfortable. I'll make you a deal: you call off your dogs and I'll call off mine."

If you do give in and give the child what he wants, you are guaranteed that any testing will stop immediately. In a split second, no more hassles. Some people say, "Thank heaven—there's a way of getting rid of testing and manipulation!" There certainly is, but what's the catch? The catch, of course, is who's running your house? It certainly isn't you; it's the kids. All they have to do during a conflict is get out their big manipulative guns and you are chopped liver.

> **Quik Tip**
> A child who is testing you is offering you a deal: give me what I want, and my badgering, temper, threat, or martyrdom will stop—immediately! Does that sound like a deal you can't refuse? Think again!

Who's Pushing Your Buttons?

Think of each of your kids, one at a time, and ask yourself, "Does this child have a favorite testing tactic? One that he or she uses very frequently or all the time?" If your answer is yes, that's bad news. Why? Because that means the testing ploy works for the child. People don't generally repeat behavior that doesn't work for them.

Let's recall the two purposes of testing and manipulation. First of all, a testing strategy works when the child successfully gets his way by using that tactic. How do you know if a child is getting his way by testing? It's obvious—you just give it to him. You give him the snack right before dinner, turn the TV back on while he's doing homework, stop counting him when he's teasing the dog, or don't make him go to bed.

> **Caution**
> Does your child have a favorite testing tactic? If your answer is yes, that means the strategy is working, either by:
> 1. getting the child her way or
> 2. allowing her to get revenge on the adult she is testing.

The idea that the testing tactic "works" can also refer to the second purpose of testing and manipulation: revenge. Children will repeat tactics that provide an effective way of retaliating against the adults who are causing the frustration. How does a child know if she is effectively getting revenge? The answer takes us right back to the No Talking, No Emotion Rules. If your child can get you very upset and get you talking too much, she knows she's got you.

Children know they are getting effective revenge when their parents say things like, "How many times do I have to tell you?" "Why can't you just take no for an answer?" "ARE YOU TRYING TO DRIVE ME NUTS?" The angry part of your frustrated child will find comments like these satisfying, and the next time your child is upset with you, he will know exactly how to press the revenge button.

Let's imagine that you want your son to do his homework, for example, and he has a tantrum (Tactic 2) because he wants to watch TV instead. If you don't follow the No Talking and No Emotion Rules, your response turns into a counter temper tantrum. You get more upset than your son did! Final score: Child 1, Parent 0. He got satisfaction from getting the angry, big splash out of the larger, "more powerful" adult.

Other kids retaliate by making their parents feel guilty. Imagine that your daughter—when asked to go to bed—resorts to martyrdom (Tactic 4): "Well, it's obvious that nobody around here loves me anymore. I might as well hitchhike to the next state and find a family more compatible with my basic needs." Here she adds a touch of threat, Tactic 3. You feel frightened and guilty. You are certain that unloved children grow up to be degenerates or serial killers. Your response is to sit your daughter down on your lap and tell her for half an hour how much you love her, how much Dad and the dog love her, and so on.

You have just been had by Tactic 4, martyrdom. You are squirming and uncomfortable, and your child is making you pay for your parenting sins. Always remember this: unless you are a grossly neglectful or abusive parent, your kids know that you love them. By all means tell them that you love them, but never tell them that when they're pulling Tactic 4 on you.

How to Manage Testing and Manipulation

Now let's say you're getting into the spirit of 1-2-3 Magic and you're toughening up some. Your ten-year-old son wants to go to a friend's house at nine on a school night. You deny his request and tell him it's too late. The following scene occurs:
"Why not? Come on, just this once!" (Badgering)
"Can't do it."
"I never get anything." (Martyrdom, badgering)
"I don't think you're too underprivileged."
"I'll clean the garage tomorrow." (Butter up, badgering)
"The garage is OK the way it is. I just cleaned it."
"This stinks—I HATE YOUR GUTS!" (Intimidation, badgering)
"Sorry."
The child throws a book on the floor. (Physical tactic)
"Watch your step, pal."
"Please, PLEASE! Oh, come on, it's not so late." (Badgering)
"No way. Not tonight."
"If you don't let me, I'm running away!" (Threat, badgering)

This interaction may be aggravating, but in a way it's good! Why? Because something constructive is happening. The child is fishing around, switching tactics and probing for your weak spot. But he can't find a weak spot. You are sticking to your guns. Not only that, but you are remaining fairly calm in spite of the aggravation.

There is one thing wrong with this example, however, and that has to do with how you handle testing and manipulation. You would not let the child switch tactics that many times (and you would also not talk so much). What should you do, then? Well, if you look at our list of six testing tactics, five of them (except butter up) are Stop behavior. As you know, Stop behavior should be counted. So if a child was pushing you this much, he should be counted.

This is how the scene should be handled using the 1-2-3 program. Remember that the boy has already been given an explanation:

"Why not? Come on, just this once!" (Badgering)
"That's 1."
"I never get anything." (Martyrdom, badgering)
"That's 2."
"I'll clean the garage tomorrow." (Butter up, badgering)
"That's 3. Take ten."

The third count is more for the badgering than the butter up, but it's obvious this kid's not going to give up until the parent gently but firmly puts his foot down. That goal is achieved by counting and the resulting BreakTime.

Remember: with the exceptions of butter up and passive pouting, testing and manipulation should be counted, especially in the beginning when you're just starting 1-2-3 Magic. Once the kids are used to the discipline system, the less aggressive, less obnoxious forms of testing can—at your discretion—occasionally be ignored. The effectiveness of not responding at all (verbally or nonverbally) to a child's testing can be evaluated by how quickly the child gives up the battle. Many kids soon learn that no response from you (ignoring) means they're not going to get their way or get effective revenge.

Which Testing Tactic Is the Most Common?

Badgering, temper, threat, martyrdom, butter up, and physical tactics are all methods children use to get their way with adults. And all these tactics, except butter up, can also be used by kids to punish the uncooperative adults who obstinately persist in refusing to give the children what they want.

We have taken several surveys of parents and teachers, asking which tactics they thought children used the most. Interestingly, both groups of grown-ups always mention the same three: badgering, temper, and—the overwhelming favorite—martyrdom.

You will also be interested to know that the most annoying manipulative maneuver used by children is a tactic that combines two of the three favorites. This tactic, which drives many parents absolutely nuts, is a combination of martyrdom (4) and badgering (1). The word describing it starts with the letter *W*. You guessed it: whining!

What to Expect in the Beginning

As we mentioned before, once you start counting, the kids will fall primarily into two categories: immediate cooperators and immediate testers. If you're lucky to have immediate cooperators, enjoy it! You will feel more affectionate toward your children because they are listening to you. You will want to have more fun with your kids, talk with them, praise them, and listen to them. You will enjoy working on building a good relationship. This good relationship, in turn, will make counting (1) less necessary and (2) a lot easier when it is necessary.

Immediate testers, however, get worse at first. When you let them know you're going to be the boss and you take away the power of their favorite testing strategies, these children deteriorate in two ways. Some will up the ante with a particular testing tactic. The volume and length of a child's tantrums, for example, may double. Badgering may become more intense or aggressive, and martyrdom may become more whiney and pathetic.

The other unpleasant change you may see initially in noncooperators is tactic switching. The kids may try manipulative strategies you haven't seen before, or they may return to others they haven't used for years. The most common switches involve going from badgering and martyrdom (and whining!) to temper. Some kids, quite understandably, blow up when their attempts to wear you down with repetition or make you feel guilty fail. Although tactic switching is aggravating, remember that switching is almost always a sign that you are doing well at sticking to your guns. Keep it up!

What do you do when you're faced with tactic escalation and tactic switching? Several things are important: (1) Don't get discouraged; this is a normal stage many children go through while adjusting to 1-2-3 Magic. (2) Count when necessary. (3) Keep your mouth shut except for necessary explanations and the counting itself. Eventually, tactic escalation and tactic switching will diminish and your children will accept your discipline without having a fit every time you have to frustrate them. You then have won the battle. You are the parent, they are the children, and your home is a more peaceful place.

> **Quik Tip**
> When in doubt, count!

One final word: after cooperating initially, some kids become "delayed testers" later. Delayed testing can occur after the novelty of the new system wears off, when the children begin to realize that they aren't getting their way anymore, or if your routine gets disrupted by travel, visitors, illness, new babies, or other factors.

If you're unprepared for it, delayed testing can be a bit disillusioning. You think to yourself, "The kids were so good before!" You may feel like the whole system is falling apart, or that it was too good to be true. Fortunately, the remedy is not far away. Read *1-2-3 Magic* again, watch the DVD, discuss the suggestions with your spouse if possible, then get back to basics. Practice No Talking, No Emotion; be gentle but aggressive; and when in doubt, count.

What to Expect Over the Years

As a parent, you naturally expect your children to take more and more responsibility for their own behavior as the years go by. That's actually what counting is all about in the first place. When you say "That's one" to a child who's whining, for example, the count means this to the child: I'm doing something wrong, I'd better figure out what it is, and I'd better stop it. The procedure is simple and gentle, and, without a lot of distracting chatter, it puts the responsibility for behavior right where it belongs—on the child's shoulders.

What will happen with counting over the years is this: you'll be counting less and less as the kids learn to manage themselves more and more. That will be a nice feeling. Once the kids are ten or eleven or so, you may go weeks or months without a single count. If the children's behavior does get a little dicey, sometimes all you will have to do is quietly say something like "I'd like this to stop or we're going to counting," and you'll see the obnoxious behavior end right away. At these ages, an explanation, however tempting it might be to you, is superfluous. Your kids know which end is up. Let them take control and keep it.

Your Child Is Keeping Track!

Your child's brain was wired from birth with many different instincts, which interact with learning over the years to produce her behavior. One natural instinct kids have is wanting to please their parents. Another instinct they have, however, is a desire to get their way—now.

These two drives often battle each other in your child's mind, and each has a large army of neurons at its disposal!

When frustrated with you (which is inevitable!), your child's brain (and a part of it called the hippocampus) will remember which testing and manipulation tactics worked in the past and which did not. What, for example, works best for getting candy right before dinner: temper, threat, or martyrdom?

CHAPTER SUMMARY
Kids' All-Time Favorite Tactic?

The 4+1 Pattern:
Whining!

11
TALES FROM THE TRENCHES
Real Stories from Real Parents

NOW LET'S STUDY SOME examples of the 1-2-3 in action to give you a feel for how and when counting can be used. Our stories and commentaries will illustrate some of the basic do's and don'ts involved with the procedure. In some of our examples, when our parents don't do so well with their discipline the first time around, we'll give them a chance to correct their mistakes. Wouldn't it be nice if you had that opportunity in real life? Guess what? You do.

Sibling Rivalry I

Round One

Like most siblings, nine-year-old John and seven-year-old Brittany are the best of friends and the worst of enemies. They are playing with Legos on the living room floor. Dad is watching the football game on TV and is amazed the kids are getting along so well, but the fun is about to end.

"Brittany, I need another wheel for my tank," says John.

"No, John, I've got it on my wagon," Brittany says.

(Dad squirms in his chair. It's fourth-and-goal for the good guys.)

"Lemme just use one wheel now. I'll give it back to you later," suggests Brother.

"No, my wagon needs four wheels," replies Sister.

"Your wagon looks stupid!"

"Dad, John's gonna take one of my wheels and I had them first!"

(Dad's team had to try for a field goal and it was blocked. Dad is not pleased.)

"Both of you, knock it off!"

"She doesn't need to hog all the wheels. There aren't enough for me to make what I want, and they're my Legos."

"But I made this first!"

"OK, kids, that's 1 for both of you."

"She's an idiot." *(John smashes his creation and leaves.)*

How Did He Do?

Pretty good discipline job by Dad. Perhaps he should have counted a little bit sooner instead of growling "Knock it off!" Should Dad have counted John for smashing his tank or bad-mouthing his sister? Some parents would count these behaviors, but others wouldn't because the tank was John's (and it can be rebuilt). John may also be doing the right thing by leaving the situation.

Round Two

Second chance: let's give Dad another chance to improve his parenting technique.

"Brittany, I need another wheel for my tank," says John.

"No, John, I've got it on my wagon," Brittany says.

(Dad squirms in his chair. It's fourth-and-goal for the good guys.)

"Lemme just use one wheel now. I'll give it back to you later," suggests Brother.

"No, my wagon needs four wheels," replies Sister.

"Your wagon looks stupid!"

"Kids, that's 1 for both of you."

(Dad's team had to try for a field goal and it was blocked. Dad is not pleased.)
"She doesn't need to hog all the wheels. There aren't enough for me to make what I want, and they're my Legos."
"But I made this first!"
"OK, kids, that's 2."

> ### How Did He Do?
> Dad did much better this time, especially since he was extra aggravated after his team blew its scoring opportunity. Excellent self-control and an excellent job of not taking out his extra frustration on the kids.

Sibling Rivalry II

Sean, nine, and Tammi, eleven, are getting into it while trying to play Scrabble in the living room. Dad is washing dishes in the kitchen.
"It's my turn."
"No it isn't. You lost it 'cause you took so long."
"Give me that. I was going to pick up that one!"
"You scratched me!"
"I did not, you idiot! You started it!"
"You're so dumb it isn't funny."
(Dad enters.) "What's going on here?"
"She's cheating!"
"I am not, lamebrain. You're too slow!"
"Be quiet, both of you! Tell me what happened."
General yelling and chaos follow the ill-fated inquiry.
"OK, that's 1 for both of you."
(General yelling and chaos continue.)
"That's 2."
Sean turns over the Scrabble board, grabs a bunch of letters, and throws them at the piano.
"Sean, that's 3. Take a rest for ten."

> **How Did He Do?**
>
> Dad recovered pretty well after beginning badly by asking the world's most ridiculous question. He should have started counting earlier.

1-2-3, Separate!

Joey, eight, and Maddie, six, are in the family room. Joey is playing with his dinosaurs, and Maddie is working on a puzzle. Janet is a single mom who is enjoying the peace and quiet while cooking dinner in the kitchen. Maddie starts humming to herself. After a few seconds, Joey asks her to stop. She says she won't. The bickering escalates.

"Joey, Maddie, that's 1," says Mom.

Both children are now on a count of 1, according to the usual sibling rivalry and counting procedure. In this situation, however, if the kids hit 3, Mom has decided that she will use a unique form of BreakTime alternative that is also a natural consequence of their actions. (See chapter 12.) The bickering continues through a count of 2, so at 3 Mom says:

"OK, guys. That's 3, separate."

This means that the children have to go to different places. They cannot be together. It's like the old bar-closing adage: "You don't have to go to your room, but you can't stay here." Both kids must leave the room they were sharing. Where they go is their choice, except that they cannot choose the same place. They may bring their toys.

> **How Did She Do?**
>
> Good creativity by this mother. Separating them is more of an interruption or redirection than a punishment. Separation can also be useful if the kids share a room and can't both go there for a break. The separation period can last the usual one minute per year of life, or it can be longer—until dinner is served, for instance. If the kids don't comply, the usual BreakTime is in order.

Trouble at the Grocery Store

Round One

Rita is four years old and loves to go shopping at the grocery store with her mom. The reason she loves shopping trips is because the store has kiddie carts she can push around just like her mother does. Rita's mom, however, does not enjoy shopping with her daughter quite as much. The reason Mom does not like these shopping trips is because sooner or later, Rita always starts running around with the cart. Last week the little girl ran into the big shopping cart of an older gentleman. Although the man was nice about it and even laughed, Mom is afraid her daughter will hurt someone.

Talk about the devil and the deep blue sea! If Mom doesn't let Rita have a cart, the girl will throw a raging fit—guaranteed—in front of everyone in the store. Mom feels her daughter is running the show.

Mom is correct. Here's how the scene goes when Mom and Rita enter the store:

"Mom! Can I push a cart?"

"I don't think so, dear. Not today. Look at the Fuzzy Bear sign!"

"Why can't I?"

"I just told you, dear. Now please don't start giving me a hard time."

"I wanna push my own one!"

"Now stop that! That's enough! Come on, we've got a lot of things to get."

"I never get to do anything!" Rita starts crying loudly.

"OK, OK! Stop that!" Mom gets a kiddie cart for Rita. She grabs the cart, but Mom holds the cart for a second and looks at her daughter firmly.

"Rita, look at me. You have to promise me you won't run with the cart. You might hurt someone. Do you understand me?"

"Yes."

"And you promise you won't run with the cart?"

"Yes."

"Say 'I promise.'"

"I promise."

"OK. Now let's get our stuff. I'll put some things in your cart."

Rita does just fine for six minutes. Then she starts running with her kiddie cart, giggling as she zooms past the spaghetti sauce. Her mother pretends she doesn't notice, but then she cuts the shopping trip short after getting only one-third of the things she needed. Maybe she can come back later and get the rest of what she wants by herself.

How Did She Do?

A classic example of a child intimidating a parent with the threat of public embarrassment. Mom is intimidated into a desperate attempt at little-adult reasoning ("You might hurt someone") and the elicitation of futile promises.

Round Two

Let's give Mom another chance to get this one right. Actually, Rita's mother has two choices: (1) counting Rita for speeding and at count 3 taking away the cart, and (2) not letting Rita have a cart in the first place.

OPTION 1: COUNTING RITA FOR SPEEDING

"Mom! Can I push a cart?"

"Yes, dear. But you have to walk with it. If I count you to 3 for running, I'll take the cart away."

Rita does fine for three minutes, then starts running with the kiddie cart.

"Rita, that's 1. At 3 you lose the cart."

How Did She Do?

This approach is much better. There will probably be hell to pay if Rita hits 3 and has her cart taken away, so Mom should be ready to take the little girl out to the car for a while until she finishes her tantrum. If returning to the car is necessary, no parental "I told you so" comments are allowed.

OPTION 2: NOT LETTING RITA HAVE THE KIDDIE CART
"Mom! Can I push a cart?"
"No. Last time you ran with it."
"Why can't I?"
"That's 1."
"I wanna push my own one!"
"That's 2."

> ### How Did She Do?
> Good work, Mom!

Dog Teasing

Four-year-old Michael has the dog backed into a corner and pushed up against the wall. The dog, normally patient, looks uncomfortable. Mom intervenes.
"Michael, please don't tease the dog, honey."
(Michael giggles and continues pushing the dog against the wall.)
"That's 1."
"No! I wanna pet him." *(For the first time, the dog snarls.)*
"That's 3. Take five. The dog is mad and could bite you."
"I WANNA PET HIM!" *(Michael falls on floor, releasing the dog, but yelling and crying. Mom carries the unwilling body to the bedroom for BreakTime.)*

> ### How Did She Do?
> Couldn't have done it better. When the dog snarled, Mom went straight to 3 because of the danger. No talking while "escorting" the child to the rest period.

Bedtime Problem

It's nine o'clock in the evening. Alex is playing an electronic game on the couch in the living room. His mother enters the room.
"Alex, it's time to get ready for bed."
(Entranced with his game, Alex does not respond at all.)
"Alex, that's 1."

> ### How Did She Do?
> Should counting be used for bedtime? No. Getting ready for bed is a Start behavior—actually, a series of Start behaviors that take a while to complete. Counting is for obnoxious behavior, such as whining, arguing, teasing, or tantrums, where cooperation takes only a few seconds. For bedtime, this mom needs a bedtime routine. (See chapter 17.)

Constant Requests

Eight-year-old Tom asks his mother if he can use his dad's electric jigsaw in the basement tool room.
"I don't think so. You better wait until Daddy's home."
"Oh come on, Mom. I know how to do it."
"No, I think it's too dangerous."
"There's nothing else to do." (Badgering, martyrdom)
"I said no. That's 1."
"THAT'S 1! THAT'S 2! THAT'S 3! THAT'S 12! THAT'S 20! THAT'S STUPID!" (Intimidation)
"That's 2."
"Didn't know you could count that high." (Intimidation)
"That's 3. Take ten and add five for the mouth."
"Gee, I'll need a calculator for this one."
Mom moves toward Tom to escort him if necessary, but he goes to his bedroom.

> **How Did She Do?**
>
> Mom did very well—one explanation and then she counted. Mom also adds five for the smart mouth, and she has the presence of mind to stay cool in spite of the insult. When her son doesn't go to the rest period right away, she also does not get caught up in an argument or little-adult conversation.

Interrupting

Round One

Mom and Dad are having a private conversation on the couch about the recent hospitalization of Mom's father. Seven-year-old Michelle jumps in between them.

"Hi, guys!"

"Hi, honey. Listen, Mom and Dad have to talk about something very important for a few minutes, so you go play for a little bit."

"I wanna be here with you. I promise I won't listen."

"No, dear. Come on now, you go and play."

"I don't have anything to do." (Badgering)

"Listen, young lady. We're not going to tell you again!"

"THERE'S NOTHING ELSE FOR ME TO DO!" (Intimidation)

"Do you want a spanking?"

(Michelle starts crying.) (Martyrdom)

"OK, that's 1."

(Michelle leaves, crying.)

> **How Did They Do?**
>
> Pretty sloppy job by Mom and Dad. In fairness to these parents, this is a touchy situation because Michelle's entrance is very friendly and these parents don't want to tell her what they're discussing just yet. They only get around to counting after ridiculous attempts at persuasion, threatening a spanking, and

> risking World War III for nothing. They eventually recover and count, but some damage has still been done.

Round Two

Second chance: let's take it from the top.

"Hi, guys!"

"Hi, honey. Listen, Mom and Dad have to talk about something very important for a few minutes, so you go play for a little bit."

"I wanna be here with you. I promise I won't listen."

"That's 1."

"I don't have anything to do." (Badgering)

"That's 2."

Michelle leaves, a bit teary.

> **How Did They Do?**
> Mom and Dad probably feel a little bit guilty, but they handled the situation well. You can't give the kids everything they want.

Arguing

As Mom is working in the kitchen after dinner, eleven-year-old Jeff asks:

"Can I go out after dinner to play?"

"No, dear, you still have homework to do," says Mom.

"I'll do it when I come back in, right before bed."

"That's what you said last night, honey, and it didn't work. Remember?"

"Oh, please Mom. I promise!" (Badgering, butter up)

"Get your homework done first, and then you can go out. If you work hard, it shouldn't take more than a half hour."

"Why can't I just go out now? I'll DO MY STUPID HOMEWORK!" (Intimidation)

"That's 1."
"I can't wait to grow up so I can go in the army. It's got to be more fun than living in this dump." (Martyrdom)
"That's 2."
"All right, all right, all right." *(Jeff goes to start his homework.)*

> **How Did She Do?**
> Mom did very well here. She tried a little negotiating, but when that didn't work, she didn't get caught up in a useless argument or try to explain why her house wasn't the same as the military.

Extreme Possessiveness

Haley is four years old. She has a playdate at her house with another little girl, Alyssa, whom she has just met. Unfortunately, everything Alyssa touches, Haley tries to take away from her. Alyssa is not aggressive at all, but just stands there looking bewildered after a new toy has been taken from her hands.

Mom sees the pattern. Alyssa picks up a small red car. Haley moves in and grabs it.

Mom says, "Haley, that's 1. You must let Alyssa play with something."
(Haley still doesn't let go.)
"Haley, that's 2."
(The little girl releases her hold and lets Alyssa have the car.)
"That's very nice of you, sweetheart."

> **How Did She Do?**
> Good job. Briefly explain, count, and praise cooperation. For the little ones we allow parents to provide a *short* explanation with the first count, for example, "No hitting. Hitting hurts people. That's 1."

Conclusion

What have our tales from the trenches taught us? Kids can certainly catch you off guard, for one thing! You have to be on your toes and—to be fair to yourself and the children—you have to make reasonable and fairly rapid decisions about which offenses are countable and which are not. Good counting takes a little bit of practice, but once you master the skill, you'll wonder how you ever got along without this sanity-saving technique.

Practice, Practice, Practice!

Practice reduces the need to think. Just like our kids need to practice and learn good behaviors, parents need to practice responding to children's behavior through the calm and decisive use of *1-2-3 Magic*. There is a shift in the brain when constructive behaviors become more automatic and less brainpower is used. Practice rewires the neurons in your brain, new pathways are formed, and your adult brain becomes more efficient as well as effective.

As the days and months progress, you will notice two changes at home, both of which are critical for the healthy growth of your child's developing brain and nervous system. First, your house will have greater emotional stability. And second, the people in your house will enjoy one another's company a lot more!

CHAPTER SUMMARY
Is it magic?

The "magic" of the 1-2-3 procedure is not in the counting itself. The power of the method comes primarily from your ability to accomplish two goals. Your first objective is to explain—when necessary—and then keep quiet. Your second objective is to count as calmly and unemotionally as you can.

Do these two things well and your children will start listening to you!

PART IV

Encouraging Good Behavior

Parenting Job 2

CHAPTER 12
Establishing Positive Routines

CHAPTER 13
Getting Up and Out in the Morning

CHAPTER 14
Cleaning Up and Chores

CHAPTER 15
Surviving Suppertime

CHAPTER 16
Tackling the Homework Problem

CHAPTER 17
Going to Bed—and Staying There!

CHAPTER 18
Managing Your Expectations

12

ESTABLISHING POSITIVE ROUTINES

How to Motivate Your Children to Do the Things They Need to Do

NOW WE TURN OUR attention to your second big parenting job: encouraging your children to do the positive things you want them to do. We call this behavior category Start behavior, because you want your children to start doing their schoolwork, going to bed, eating their supper, cleaning their rooms, and getting up and out in the morning.

Recall that Start behavior requires more motivation from children than Stop behavior. While it may take only one second to stop whining or arguing, tasks such as doing homework or getting off to school may require thirty minutes or more. Kids not only have to start these jobs, they also have to continue and finish them. Counting difficult behavior is fairly easy. When it comes to encouraging positive behavior, however, moms and dads have to be more skilled motivators.

When they're beginning 1-2-3 Magic, most parents use counting to manage Stop behavior for a week to ten days before tackling Start behavior. If you try to do the whole program at once (both Stop and Start problems), it may be confusing or take too much energy. Equally important, it will be a lot easier to get the kids to do the good things if they know you have gotten back in control of the house by effectively managing their obnoxious conduct.

When you begin using your Start behavior tactics, don't be surprised if you run into testing and manipulation. Your daughter may not thank you for training her to clean her room. If you have worked on counting negative behavior first, you will have had a fair amount of experience in dealing with Stop behavior before you tackle the task of getting the kids to do the good things—so have your counting strategy ready in your back pocket.

> **Quik Tip**
>
> With Start behavior, you can use more than one tactic at a time for a particular problem. You may even come up with some of your own strategies. Remember: train your kids to do what you want, or keep quiet!

In dealing with Start behavior, keep in mind one of the basic rules of 1-2-3 Magic: train the children or keep quiet! The 1-2-3 program includes a method for handling just about every kind of problem your kids can throw at you. So use these methods! Kids, for example, are not born to be natural room cleaners. If the child isn't cleaning his room, train him to clean it. Otherwise, be quiet, clean it yourself, or close the door and don't look. Training does not mean nagging, arguing, yelling, or hitting.

Wonderful, Powerful Routines!

Many people think the word "routine" means bad and boring. You will soon learn that when it comes to Start behavior, routines are wonderful and powerful. Activities like homework and going to bed are complex and take time. Kids have to learn to regularly follow a fixed sequence of actions. Same time, same place, same way. Once a routine is mastered, kids tend to do it automatically.

Routines for positive behavior drastically reduce your discipline problems, and they can also make testing and manipulation virtually nonexistent. We'll discuss more about how to establish routines at the end of this chapter.

Dealing with Toddlers

In establishing routines, you'll find that toddlers (ages one to three or so) will respond well to several of our Start behavior strategies, while others will be over their heads a bit. Toddlers do well, for example, with praise, simple requests, and the counting variation, and some three-year-olds can begin to understand simple timers and simple charts. Digital timers, the docking system, natural consequences, and charting, however, may be less useful for getting these kids started with positive behavior.

What to do? You'll find that there are a lot of other tactics that toddlers do respond well to. These kids, for example, are great imitators. So how do you get a toddler to brush her teeth? Modeling that behavior yourself is a great start. Other toddler-oriented methods can include things like choice—let a child choose her clothes or toothbrush or toothpaste. Making the activity fun with music or other diversions can also help, and so can friendly challenges such as "Do you know how to do this?" Letting the child control as much of the activity as possible also facilitates cooperation. In addition, you'll find lots of books as well as YouTube videos that portray kids engaging in daily routines such as eating, going to bed, brushing teeth, and getting dressed.

Keeping training sessions brief and not insisting on perfection are also useful ways of maximizing children's motivation. When it comes to toddlers and Start behaviors, a fun and creative approach goes a long way toward keeping both children and parents constructively involved in the new learning.

The Seven Start Behavior Tactics

There are seven Start behavior tactics that you can consider using to establish and maintain your routines. Sometimes you may use just one tactic, but other times you may use two or three for the same problem. While counting obnoxious behavior is fairly straightforward, you can be more creative and flexible in managing positive behavior. In fact, many parents and teachers have come up with useful and imaginative ideas that are not on our list.

Here are our seven strategies for encouraging good behavior:

1. Positive reinforcement
2. Simple requests
3. Kitchen timers
4. The docking system
5. Natural consequences
6. Charting
7. Counting variation

With these rules in mind, let's take a look at the seven tactics you will use to get the kids to do what they're supposed to.

1. Positive Reinforcement

Why is there a home-field advantage in sports? It's because the crowd encourages their team by cheering and applauding. Even for adult professional athletes, this type of praise is a strong motivator. Unfortunately, the effect of this home-field advantage doesn't always translate from stadium to home. Why?

Angry people make noise; happy people keep quiet. That's why. We all suffer from a biological curse that motivates us to say something to our kids when we're angry at them, but to keep quiet when the little ones are doing what we want them to do. Imagine it's a Sunday in October and I'm watching a football game in the afternoon. My two children are in the next room playing a game together, having a great time, and getting along very well. What do you think the chances are that I'm going to get up out of my chair, walk all the way into the next room, and say, "Gee, I'm delighted you guys are having such a good time!" That would be a great thing, but the chances of my doing it are about zero. Why? Because when adults are happy and content themselves, they are not particularly motivated to do anything more than what they're already doing.

But imagine that my children in the next room start fighting and screaming. Why do they behave this way? I can't even hear the football game! Now I am motivated—I'm mad. Now the chances of my getting up, running into the other room, and yelling at the kids to keep quiet are high. Anger is a much better motivator than contentment. The result is that our kids are more likely to hear from us when we have negative rather than positive feedback.

One powerful antidote to this unfortunate natural inclination is praise, or positive verbal reinforcement. Your praise and other positive interactions with your kids should outnumber your negative comments by a ratio of about three to one. If you look, you shouldn't have trouble finding some positive behavior to reinforce:

"Thanks for doing the dishes."
"You started your homework all by yourself!"
"That dog really likes you."
"You kids did a good job of getting along during the movie."
"I think you got ready for school in record time this morning!"
"Good job on that math test, John."
"I saw you out on the soccer field. You played hard—good hustle!"
"That's wonderful! I can't believe it! How on earth did you do that?"

Once the kids are successfully carrying out a particular Start behavior routine, praise can help keep the cooperation or good performance going. Many parents, for example, praise or thank their kids for complying with simple requests or for following a bedtime or homework routine.

Keep a sensitive eye on your son or daughter, though, because praise should be tailored to each child and each situation. Some kids like rather elaborate, syrupy, and emotional verbal reinforcement, while others do not. Imagine, for example, your eight-year-old daughter getting 100 percent on her spelling test. You say, "Oh, Melissa, that's just marvelous! I can't believe it! We're going to frame this and overnight a copy of it to Grandma in Florida!" Melissa eats it up.

However, Melissa's eleven-year-old brother would be nauseated by that kind of talk. For him, "Good job—keep up the good work," and a pat on the shoulder might be enough. Your job is to praise the child, not to embarrass him. The long and short of it is: if your child enjoys praise, then by all means provide it—when appropriate.

> **Quik Tip**
> Are we spoiling our kids with superficial, phony praise? Basically, you can give elaborate praise to kids younger than seven—they likely can't tell the difference between fake and genuine praise. Once kids get older than that, it's best to dial back on the praise and make sure that you're only giving them genuine, heartfelt compliments.

The tactic of praise sometimes gets criticized for being overused and abused. People say we spoil our children with exaggerated compliments, artificially inflate their self-esteem, and consequently don't prepare them for the big, bad world. Is this a real problem?

Here's the deal. With kids up to age about five or six, it's not so bad to exaggerate your praise of their effort or their performance. They respond positively to almost any kind of encouragement, and they don't always really know how well or poorly they are doing. But watch out when those kids hit first or second grade! Now they are starting to get an idea of what doing well really means, and they will increasingly be able to tell fake from genuine praise.

There are two additional devices you can use to make praise a more effective boost to a child's self-esteem:

1. Praise in front of other people
2. Unexpected praise

While you're talking to your next-door neighbor, for example, your daughter Kelsey shows up. You interrupt your conversation and say, "You should have seen Kelsey out there on the soccer field today. Those other kids never knew what hit them!" Kelsey will beam with pride.

Unexpected praise can also be quite memorable for a child. Your son is upstairs doing his homework. You call from the bottom of the stairs, "Hey, Jordan!" Jordan has no idea what's coming next. You then say, "Did I tell you what a great job you did on the yard?" Jordan will be pleased—and perhaps a little relieved!

How do you keep offering praise and encouragement on a regular basis? As mentioned before, this task is surprisingly difficult, since most of us tend not to speak up when we are content. Here are two suggestions. First, see if you can make three positive comments for every negative one (and, by the way, a count is one negative comment). These positive remarks don't have to be made at the same time, of course. They can be made later. If the three-to-one ratio idea doesn't appeal to you, a second strategy is to have a quota system. Each day you make a deal with yourself that you will make at least five positive comments to each child (and consider doing the same with your spouse).

Make sure your kids get the home-field advantage!

2. Simple Requests

The problem with simple requests is that they are not so simple. Parental requests to children can be made more or less effective by the parent's tone of voice, the spontaneity of the request, and the phrasing of the demand.

We all have different voices. When she was younger, my daughter had several different variations of the simple expression, "Dad!" One "Dad!" meant "I'm excited and want to show you something." Another "Dad!" meant "I want assistance because my brother is teasing me." And yet a third "Dad!" (during her teen years) meant, "Cool it, old-timer, you're embarrassing me in public!"

Parents have different voices too. The voice we're concerned about here is called "chore voice." Chore voice has a quality of "You're not doing what I expect and it's really irritating and what's the matter with you and when are you going to learn…" and so on. Chore voice has an aggravated, nagging, and anxious tone that most children find annoying. When this parental tone of voice is coupled with a request, it makes cooperation less likely because you are now asking an angry child to cooperate.

A good antidote to chore voice is a businesslike, matter-of-fact presentation. "John, it is now time to start your homework" or "Taylor, bedtime." This tone of voice implies, "You may not like this, but it's got to be done now." Testing is much less likely when requests are made in a matter-of-fact way, but—believe it or not—the mere tone of voice can also say, "If you test or push me, you'll get counted."

Quik Tip
Try not to spring unpleasant requests on your kids out of the blue. Giving them a little warning will usually help them do what you want—with less whining!

The spontaneity of a parental request can also be a cooperation killer. Your son is outside playing baseball with some friends. You go to the front door and ask him if he'd come in and take out the garbage. He blows his stack and you think, "What is the big deal?" You are correct that your boy overreacted, but the big deal was not the garbage. The big deal to him was the spontaneity. What do you expect the child to say? "Thanks for offering me this opportunity to be of service to the family"?

No one likes spur-of-the-moment interruptions that involve unpleasant tasks. You don't like them either, although you are often stuck with such intrusions. But we're not talking about getting you to cooperate here. We're talking about getting your kids to cooperate. And we're also not saying your children shouldn't have chores to do. They should help out around the house. Structure these tasks into fixed routines so that spontaneous requests are seldom necessary.

Finally, the phrasing of a request can make a difference in how kids respond. Phrasing a request as a question and adding the ridiculous "we" to the statement will often ensure noncompliance or testing and manipulation. A supersweet "Don't we think it's about time to start our homework?" for example, is almost guaranteed to elicit a negative response. "I want your schoolwork complete by five o'clock" is better.

What if, in spite of everything, your simple request still does no good? We'll come back to that question at the end of this chapter after we've discussed several other Start behavior options.

3. Kitchen Timers

Kitchen timers are wonderful devices for encouraging good behavior in children. Many kinds are useful, including the sixty-minute wind-up variety as well as computer, small LCD, and even hourglass varieties. The people who manufacture timers think they're for baking cakes. They're not—timers are for raising kids! Kitchen timers can be a great help for just about any Start behavior routine, whether it's picking up, feeding the fish, getting up in the morning, taking out the garbage, or going to bed. Kids, especially the younger ones, have a natural tendency to want to beat a ticking mechanical device. The problem then becomes a case of man against machine (rather than child against parent).

These portable motivational gadgets can also be used, if you like, to time the BreakTimes themselves. Many kids actually prefer doing the rest periods with a timer. You can also take timers in the car with you and use them—as we'll see later—to help control sibling rivalry. Timers can be part of routines for bedtime or bath time or getting up and out in the morning.

Timers also can soften the blow of unavoidable spontaneous requests. A friend of yours calls and says she'll be over in fifteen minutes. You say to your five-year-old daughter, "You've got three things in the kitchen I would like picked up and put in your room. I'm setting the timer for ten minutes, and I'll bet you can't beat it!"

Her response will often be, "Oh yes I can!" as she hurries off to do the job. You could use this same approach to get an eleven-year-old to pick up, but you would phrase your request in a more matter-of-fact manner. If the child doesn't respond before the timer dings, you can use the docking system (see strategy 4) or a version of natural consequences (see strategy 5).

Kitchen timers are also effective because they are not testable. Machines cannot be emotionally manipulated. Imagine that you had to remind your son to call his grandmother to thank her for the birthday present she mailed. Your son balks, so you set the timer for ten minutes. The boy's response is "This is stupid!" (Testing Tactic 2, temper). Your response is silence. The timer's response is tick, tick, tick.

4. The Docking System

The principle of docking wages is this: if you don't do the work, you don't get paid. The basic idea of the docking system is similar: if you don't do the work, I'll do it for you— and you'll pay me. The docking system is for children who are kindergarten age or above.

This plan, of course, requires that the kids first have a source of funds from an allowance, work around the house, birthday gifts, or some other financial reservoir. You can consider starting an allowance with children who are about five years old or more. The payment doesn't have to be anything large, but it's a good idea to have half of it based on completing jobs around the house (for example, cleaning the bedroom, chores, homework). The other half is simply given to the child because he is part of the family—and also so you have some leverage when it comes time to use the docking procedure.

Let's imagine you've been having discussions with your nine-year-old son about getting a dog. Your son wants the dog, but you wisely object that you're concerned he won't feed it and take care of it properly. Let's assume you get the dog (partly because you want one too).

You then tell the child what the deal will be. He gets an allowance of about three dollars per week. You want the dog fed before six each night. If he feeds the dog then, fine. If he forgets to feed the dog before six, you have good news and bad news. The good news is that you will feed the dog for the boy. The bad news is that you charge to feed other people's dogs, and for this mutt it will be fifteen cents per feeding taken off your son's three-dollar allowance. The child readily agrees, since he's so happy about getting the dog to begin with.

Here's how events might play out. The first night you're in the kitchen making dinner. It's six ten, there's no one around, and the dog's hungry. You wait. At six fifteen your son comes running in asking if you fed the dog. You say, "No." He says, "Good!" and feeds the dog. You praise the boy, "Hey, great job! That dog was sure happy to see you."

The second night you're in the kitchen and it's six twenty. The dog is looking hungry, but you wait. Now it's six thirty and the dog is licking your legs! So you finally feed the hungry animal. At six forty your boy comes running in:

"Did you feed the dog?"

"Yes, I did. I charged you fifteen cents from your allowance."

"WELL, WHAT DID YOU DO THAT FOR?" (Yelling)

"That's 1."

This is not a discussion. It was a discussion, but now it's an attack. It's simply one version of Testing Tactic 2, temper, and it should be counted. You discuss discussions and you count attacks. In this kind of situation, it's extremely difficult to resist the temptation to get into angry, little-adult types of comments, such as, "Do you remember when we bought this stupid animal for you? What did you say? You said, 'I'll feed the dog every single night. No problem!' Right! Well, here we are on only the second night and I'm already feeding your dog! I'm sick of doing everything around here for all you people!"

What you're saying may be absolutely correct, but tirades like this will do no good. Parental tantrums and righteous indignation will, in fact, cause harm. Your tirade will do two things. First, the outburst will damage your relationship with your child. Second, your blow-up will ruin the effect of the boy having his allowance docked. So be quiet and let the money do the talking. If money doesn't seem to have much clout with this particular child, take minutes off TV, game, or computer time, or use some other reasonable consequence.

The docking system is good for lots of things. How many times have you had the feeling that parenting is unfair? About nine million times? This unfairness applies especially to the moms, who often feel they get stuck with all the extra chores around the house. Well, think of this. Now, if you are going to have to do all that stuff, you're going to get paid for it!

Have you ever said to your kids, for example, "I'm happy to do your laundry on Saturday. All you have to do is get your clothes down to the washer by nine. But I'll be darned if I'm going to go up to your room every weekend to get your dirty underwear out from underneath your bed!"

> **Quik Tip**
> With the docking system, you tell the kids, "I have good news and bad news. The good news is that if you forget a chore, I'll do it for you. The bad news is that you're going to pay me for helping you out." Then tell them the exact amount they will have to pay you.

Now let's imagine you're going to use the docking system for laundry. You say this: "I'm happy to do your laundry on Saturday mornings. All you have to do is get your clothes down to the washer by nine. If you don't get your clothes down by then, I will go up to your room to get your dirty things. But I charge for that service. And for a pile the size of the one you usually have, it will probably cost you seventy-five cents to a dollar."

5. Natural Consequences

With natural consequences you let the big, bad world teach the child what works and what doesn't. There are times when staying out of the problem is the best approach. Suppose you have a fourth grader who is taking piano lessons for the first time. She is not practicing as she should and can't sleep at night because she's worrying that her piano teacher will be mad.

What should you do? Nothing right away. See if the natural consequence of not practicing (teacher's displeasure) will alter your daughter's behavior. Some piano teachers are very good at getting uncooperative kids to tickle the ivories on a regular basis between lessons. If after a few weeks the teacher's efforts don't work, you may want to try other Start behavior tactics, such as using the timer or charting.

Or, suppose you have a boy in the sixth grade. Because you're in a hurry every morning, part of his before-school routine is making his own lunch, with goods that you buy, and then brown-bagging it to school. It seems like every other day he is telling you how hungry he was at lunch because he forgot to pack his food.

What should you do? Relax, don't lecture, and leave the responsibility squarely on his shoulders. Let the natural consequence (his empty stomach) talk to him instead of his mother talking to him. Give him some encouragement by saying something like this: "I'm sure you'll do better tomorrow."

Another example of a good time to use natural consequences? The wintertime dress of preteens and adolescents. All parents know that middle school and high school students think there are federal laws against zipping or buttoning up their coats in the winter. These kids do not want to look like their mothers dressed them in the morning. The solution? Let the cold talk to the kids if they're not dressed properly, and avoid starting the day with the obvious, aggravating comment, "You're not going out like that again, are you?"

> **Caution**
> Natural reinforcers, such as praise, sometimes aren't enough to motivate children to complete a task—especially if the kids hate the job! In these cases artificial rewards can be used. Try to borrow some motivation from somewhere else. It works!

Here's one final, real-life example of natural consequences. A mother I used to see years ago had a four-year-old boy who was driving her nuts in the morning. The boy was in preschool, but he wouldn't get dressed on time for his car-pool ride. Every morning when the horn honked in the driveway, this little guy was sitting in his pajamas watching cartoons on TV. The poor mom was tearing her hair out.

One morning she decided she'd had enough. The boy was in his pajamas watching cartoons when the car in the drive honked. Mom then calmly sent her son off to school in his pajamas. The child spent three hours with his peers while wearing little flowered booties and with butterflies all over his chest. At our next session a relieved mom reported to me that, since that day, she never again had a problem with her son being ready for his ride.

6. Charting

Charting is a very friendly motivational technique. With charting you use something like a calendar to keep track of how well a child is doing with different Start behavior routines. You can put the chart on the refrigerator door, if public acclaim is desired, or on the back of the child's bedroom door, if privacy is desired. The days of the week usually go across the top of the chart, and

down the left side is a list of the tasks the child is working on, such as picking up after herself, getting to bed, and clearing the table after supper. If the child completes the task to your satisfaction, you indicate this on the chart with stickers for the little kids (approximate ages four to nine) and grades or points (A–F, 5–1) for the older children.

A typical chart, for example, might have three to five items on it—nothing too complicated, but satisfying to complete.

With charting, positive reinforcement comes, we hope, from three things: the chart itself, parental praise, and the inherent satisfaction of doing a good job. We call these three things natural reinforcers. When my daughter was nine, she decided she wanted to take piano lessons. Although this was her choice, she didn't practice regularly and—like the fourth-grader we mentioned earlier—she worried a lot the night before her lesson that her teacher was going to be upset with her when she couldn't perform well.

We first tried natural consequences, suggesting to our little girl that she work out the problem with her teacher. This tactic failed. So we next tried charting with only natural reinforcers. Our agreement was this: Each day after practicing, our daughter was to find her mother or father and tell that parent exactly how many minutes she had practiced. One of us would then write that number for that day on the chart and praise our budding concert pianist for her work. That was it. The plan worked like a charm.

Unfortunately for parents, natural reinforcers are frequently insufficient to motivate a child to complete a particular task. Your son, for example, may simply be a natural slob—a clean room means nothing to him. Or your little girl may have ADHD and be learning-disabled, so homework provides no satisfaction—but much frustration—for her.

In these cases you must use what we call artificial reinforcers. These are things that the child will earn for successful completion of a task. The reinforcers may have nothing directly to do with the given task. But since the activity doesn't offer any incentive to the child—and, in fact, may provide a negative incentive—we are going to try to borrow motivation from somewhere else. The little girl who hates homework, for example, might earn part of her allowance, a special meal, or a special time with you.

For smaller children, the best ideas are often relatively small things that can be dished out frequently in little pieces. With older kids, larger rewards that take longer to earn become more feasible. Let yourself be creative in coming up with reinforcers. Rewards certainly do not always have to be material. Some kids, for example, will work hard to earn minutes to stay up later at night or to be able to do a special activity with one of their parents.

My daughter used what she called a "sticker book" with her three- and five-year-olds. She folded three sheets of colored construction paper together and put two staples in the crease. The child's name then went on the cover along with some decorations. Then she went sticker shopping with the kids and got stickers each of them liked. Whenever the child then completed a Start behavior, he or she got to choose a sticker and put it in the book. The kids were proud of their books.

Possible Artificial Reinforcers

- A trip for ice cream
- Brightly colored tokens
- A small toy
- Renting a special game
- Outing with a parent
- Shopping trip
- Sleepover
- Playing a game with a parent
- A no-chore voucher
- Camping out in the backyard
- Card for a collection
- Tech time
- Breakfast in bed
- Cash
- Staying up past bedtime
- Renting a special movie
- A grab-bag surprise

- Comic book or magazine
- Friend over for supper
- Choice of three reinforcers
- Reading a story with parents
- Sleeping with the dog or cat
- Special phone call
- Other items for collections
- Helping make and eat cookies
- Using a power tool with supervision

Keep charts simple. Three or four things to work on at one time are enough; more than that get too confusing. I saw a family once who created a chart for their son on which they were attempting to rate thirty-three different behaviors every day! I had to give them an A for effort, but also a high rating for confusion.

Keep in mind that you probably will not want to do charting for long periods of time. Charting can become a semi-obnoxious behavioral accounting task, and the positive effects can fade when Mom and Dad become tired of filling out the chart every day. So build in "discontinuation criteria"—rules for determining when the chart is no longer necessary.

You might say, for example, that if the child gets good scores (define this precisely) for two weeks running on a particular behavior, that item will be taken off the chart. When the child has earned his way off the chart entirely, it's time to go out for pizza and a movie to celebrate. If after a while the child doesn't keep up with the desired behavior, you can reinstate the chart.

7. Counting Variation: Brief Start Behavior

As mentioned earlier, one of the most frequent mistakes parents make with the 1-2-3 program is attempting to use counting to get a child to do Start behavior like homework, chores, or getting up and out in the morning. Recall that these tasks can take twenty minutes or more, while counting itself only produces several seconds' worth of motivation.

What if the Start behavior itself only required a few seconds' worth of cooperation? You want your daughter to hang up her coat, feed the cat, or come into the room. Counting, which is so useful for Stop behavior, can be used for some Start behavior, but only on one condition: what you want the child to do cannot take more than about two minutes. For example, your child throws her coat on the floor after school, and you ask her to pick it up. She doesn't, and you say, "That's 1." If she still refuses to comply and gets timed out, she goes and serves the time. When she comes out, you say, "Would you please hang up your coat?" If there is still no cooperation, another time-out would follow.

What if this girl, for some unknown reason, is in a totally ornery mood today and never seems to get the idea? With Start behavior tactics you have more flexibility. Switch from counting to the docking system and the kitchen timer. Set the timer for five minutes and tell your daughter she has that time to hang up the coat. If she does pick it up, fine. You promise you'll not say another word.

If she doesn't hang the thing up, however, you have good news and bad news. You'll hang up the coat for her, but you will charge for your services. The charge will be twenty-five cents for the coat and twenty-five cents for all the aggravation involved in getting her to hang it up. Keep the talking to a minimum, and count whining, arguing, yelling, and other forms of testing.

What can you use this version of the 1-2-3 for? Items like brushing teeth, picking up something, or just "Would you please come here for a second?" You are in the kitchen and you need some help for a minute. You can see your ten-year-old son in the other room, lying on the couch, eyes wide open. You say, "Would you please come here?" His response is "I can't. I'm busy."

This kid's about as busy as a rock. So let's redo this one.

"Would you please come here?"

"I can't. I'm busy."

"That's 1."

"Oh, all right!"
And the reluctant servant enters the room to carry out your bidding.

Simple Requests Revisited

Now let's return to our question about simple requests. What if, in spite of the fact that your voice quality was matter-of-fact, your request was not spur-of-the-moment, and your phrasing was not wishy-washy, your child still does not comply with what you ask him to do? After reading this chapter, you should now see that you have several options.

For example, after your son returned home from school, you told him: "Be sure you change your clothes before you go outside to play." He's having a snack and playing an electronic game, still in his school clothes, when one of his friends calls him from the back door. Your son calls back that he'll be right out. It doesn't sound as though a different wardrobe is on his mind at all.

Here are some choices you have at this point:

1. Set the timer for ten minutes and tell your son, "I want your clothes changed before the timer goes off." Avoid what we call "shouldy" thinking—the kind of parental thinking that expects kids to act like adults. If you were into shouldy thinking, you might have said, "I want your clothes changed before the timer goes off. I already told you that. What does it take to get you to listen to me for once? I'm the one who has to do the laundry, you know, and buy you all sorts of new things to wear!"

   You could also add a reward or a consequence to the act of changing clothes before the timer goes off. You would not do this every time, but sometimes a strategy like this can jump-start the kids into remembering a new behavior. "If you change before the timer goes off, you can stay up ten minutes later tonight. If you don't beat the timer, bedtime is ten minutes earlier." Simple, calm, straightforward.

2. Can you use the docking system here? No, because you can't dress him and charge him for the service. You could, of course, use the docking system if what you had asked your son to do was take out the garbage. After his first refusal of the refuse, you might simply say, "Do you want to take out the trash, or do you want to pay me to do it?" Good maneuver.
3. How about natural consequences for our reluctant clothes changer? This tactic is a possibility. The boy who plays outside in his school clothes might be required to wash his outfit as soon as he comes in.
4. Finally, you could consider using counting. Can your son change clothes in two minutes? Maybe. So as the boy is walking out the door—school outfit still on—you simply say, "That's 1." He probably won't know right away what you're talking about, so he'll respond with, "What?" His comment may even be a little ornery.

That's good—make him think a little. You pause, then say, "School clothes." If your son then goes off to his room in a huff to change, fine. You probably don't have to count the huff. If, however, he yells at you, "*Why do I always have to change my idiot school clothes? Are they made out of gold threads?*"

Pop quiz: What should you do now?
You got it! You say, "That's 2" for Testing Tactic 2, temper.

Getting Started: Rehearsing Your Routines

These are some of the tactics you can use to help set up your routines with the kids. The better a routine, the less aggravation and the less motivation is required when the kids have to produce the required behavior. The sign of a good routine is that your prompting and nagging are minimal, and your comments mostly involve positive reinforcement.

It's a good idea to practice the routines once you've defined them.

Simply defining a routine and then expecting the kids to comply without any rehearsals is the Little Adult Assumption at work in your brain again. Kids need to see, feel, and remember how the particular routine works. So make time for some leisurely dress rehearsals of your Start behavior routines—before the procedure actually needs to be used.

With the little ones (under five years old) you can use a model-and-pretend method for practicing. You say something like this: "Let's practice getting ready for bed. Isn't that silly? The sun is still shining! What do we have to do to get ready?" Then reinforce the kids' positive answers.

Next you describe the process as you model the procedure for them. "First, I'm going to wash up—just like you said. Then I'm going to put my jammies on (put something over your clothes). Next we sit on the bed for a story."

After you've modeled the routine, have the child do it and praise her as she goes along: "That's it—you remembered what was next. Good work." Remember, some kids like business and some syrup!

With older kids (five and up), you can skip the modeling and just ask them to go through the motions. Praise the kids and suggest modifications in what they are doing as necessary.

Once you've rehearsed your routines and started using them, try to keep pretty much to the same time, same place, same way. But what if the kids get sloppy with their homework or bedtime routine? Remember Start Behavior Tactic 5—natural consequences? A natural consequence of getting sloppy with a routine is needing to rehearse and practice the routine again! No righteous indignation, nagging, or arguing from you is necessary. Be nice and praise cooperation. You'll find that things will fall back into place.

That's our list of Start behavior strategies. You'll probably be able to come up with several of your own after a while. Next we'll take a look at how to apply these tactics to some of the most common Start behavior problems. But before we do that, we have to deal with one piece of unfinished business. When it comes to positive behavior, it's one thing for children to cooperate with your commands, prompts, and reminders. Compliance and cooperation with parents are a necessary step in the process of kids growing up, but they're not our ultimate goal. Our ultimate goal is kids becoming self-starters and managing their behavior themselves. In other words, we have to get you out of the picture!

Start Behavior and Executive Functioning

You hear a lot these days about what is called "executive functioning." Executive functioning involves *self-control*, and you might think of it as the ability to execute a plan or to do a job. To carry out a plan or do a job (like a Start behavior), you have to be able to do several things:

1. Remember what the job is.
2. Perform the steps required for the job in the right order.
3. Avoid getting sidetracked.

As humans get older, they usually increase their ability to successfully carry out longer and more complex plans. This ability *includes activities they are not always particularly interested in doing*, such as getting up and out in the morning, going to bed, or doing homework. If we take homework as an example, here is a chart describing children's approximate capacities at different ages for doing independent school work:

- Age 6: 10 minutes
- Age 7: 20 minutes
- Age 8: 30 minutes
- Age 9: 40 minutes

If you have a seven-year-old in his bedroom doing homework, for instance, you might want to check him after twenty minutes to see if he's still on task. A nine-year-old, on the other hand, might last forty minutes with no adult direction or reminders. This list will give you a rough idea of what other kinds of not-always-interesting activities kids might be able to carry off at different ages.

Who Can Do What?

This executive functioning model can help us to answer two of the most common email and Facebook questions we get:

1. Why can't my three-year-old clean up her room?
2. With regard to positive behavior, at what age can my kids fend for themselves? Why do I have to tell them to do everything?

What's the answer to the first question? The answer is because she's only three! Toddlers are very distractible. Even tasks that take only a few minutes, such as brushing teeth, getting dressed, or going potty, can be difficult for them to carry out. If these tasks are part of a larger sequence called "Getting up and out in the morning," toddlers may be lost. They forget what they're supposed to be doing, they get their sequences mixed up, and they get distracted playing with the dog.

According to our executive functioning chart, even a six-year-old can last only about ten minutes while doing a semi-interesting task. Most of our Start behaviors, like getting up and out, cleaning up, chores, and going to bed, fall into that category. So toddlers and preschoolers will need more or less constant support (praise and guidance) while doing these activities. We can't take you out of the picture yet with these age groups.

But what about the second question: When can children do things independently? Look at our list of Start behaviors. Next, check out the executive functioning capacity of a typical nine-year-old in our chart (forty minutes or so), and what do you get? A typically developing nine-year-old can do all that stuff! And if we wanted them to, they could also prepare meals, do interior cleaning, do laundry, and clean up the kitchen. But we don't let them do it, and we don't train them to do it. We have fallen into a pattern of chronic supervision.

We chatter at the kids and constantly oversee their activities, whether they need this "assistance" or not.

How to Really Get Out of the Picture

So it appears we have a huge amount of untapped potential in our kids. The executive functioning abilities of children after about fourth grade are pretty good! Not only that, kids want to handle themselves independently, they want to do what the big people are doing, and they want to contribute to the common family welfare. So consider the following:

1. Set up your Start behavior routines, then, when the kids are a bit older, get yourself out of the routine by eliminating your prompts, reminders, and supervision.
2. Consider using natural consequences where applicable. See the Up and Out in the Morning example for older kids in chapter 13.
3. When using charting, add that extra "magic" point for *starting on your own without being reminded*. See chapter 16.
4. Analyze your spontaneous supervisory chatter with the kids. Look closely at their reaction. Does your talk help or make things worse?
5. Ask your children in approximately third and fourth grades to do meaningful household tasks, such as laundry, food prep, kitchen clean up, shopping, and housecleaning. We often forget that these tasks can be enjoyable for many people (including kids!), and we also forget that *it's satisfying for humans to contribute to the common welfare*. Don't focus so much on less important activities that contribute little to the common good, such as baking cookies, cleaning bedrooms, or completing a weekend chore list of trivial tasks.

Parents enjoy seeing their children behaving independently and competently. Such behavior inspires affection and pride in adults. More important than that, kids are proud of themselves when they operate that way!

Independence and Self-Esteem

In general, the brain's reward system, which includes parts of the hypothalamus, is activated when it feels good. When the brain feels good, it wants to have that feeling again. This process is called learning. We learn patterns of behavior by feeling good about them. Kids' brains are hardwired to feel good about being able to operate more and more independently from their parents. We call this self-esteem.

Routines are a great brain trick. When you use positive routines and do things in the same way over and over again, you actually use deeper brain structures, such as the cerebellum, or "little brain." When kids get into routines, they don't tire out their brains as much. Instead, no thinking is required. When no thinking is needed, kids just do. And they do more than you ever thought they could.

CHAPTER SUMMARY
Your Seven Start Behavior Tactics

1. Positive reinforcement
2. Simple requests
3. Kitchen timers
4. The docking system
5. Natural consequences
6. Charting
7. Counting variation

Keep your thinking cap on—and good luck!

13
GETTING UP AND OUT IN THE MORNING

Building the Routines That Start Your Day

IF EVER A ROUTINE was sorely needed, it's for getting the kids up and out of the house in the morning. This is a problem for grammar-school kids, but it can also be an issue for preschoolers, high school students, and even spouses. Morning often brings out the worst in everybody. Many people—both parents and kids—are naturally crabby at this point, and there is the additional strain of having to get someplace on time. The pressure, nervousness, and emotional thunderstorms that can result have ruined many a parent's day.

For the kids, the morning routine involves a whole sequence of Start behaviors: (1) getting out of bed; (2) bathroom, washing up, and brushing teeth; (3) getting dressed; (4) eating breakfast; and (5) leaving the house on time with the right equipment. What is required may vary some from family to family (like switching 3 and 4), but it's basically the same job.

Believe it or not, these stressful morning situations can often be shaped up rather quickly using some of the Start behavior principles we just outlined. Remember, on school day mornings, counting will not be your primary tactic. And the No Talking and No Emotion Rules still apply—even if you haven't had your first cup of coffee.

Before you design your morning routine, a few pieces of advice may help. First, do as much preparation as you can the night before (packing book bags, selecting clothes, planning breakfast). Second, try to get up fifteen minutes before the kids. (Older children may give you more snooze time.) And third, keep breakfast simple, quick, and healthy.

Getting Up and Out for the Little Kids

Small children in the two-to-five-year-old range are going to need a lot of help and supervision in the morning. These children are not capable of sustaining a positive activity for more than a few minutes, and most of them will not even think of what needs to be done to get out of the house. You're going to have to help two- and three-year-olds get dressed and wash up. Try to do things in the same order every day. You'll also be responsible for remembering anything the children have to take with them. And while you're doing all this, you'll want to praise whatever positive efforts they make.

Four- and five-year-olds will often respond to the use of very primitive, basic charts. The chart may have only two or three items on it. These charts can be combined with kitchen timers to produce an effective motivational system. A chart for a preschooler might look something like this:

	MON	TUES	WED	THURS	FRI
OUT OF BED					
BRUSH TEETH					
GET DRESSED					

Set the timer for fifteen minutes and give the child a cue that it's time to get started. Many of the little ones are already out of bed, so that item on the chart has been successfully completed. Whichever other tasks the child finishes before the timer goes off are recognized with special stickers.

With kids in the primary grades, the chart may have all the morning-routine items on it and the timer may or may not be necessary. For each task, the child earns her favorite sticker for a super job and her next favorite sticker for a good job. No sticker at all means "You blew it today, better luck tomorrow!" The application of the stickers, of course, should be accompanied by a lot of praise: "Good job!" or "Wow, you did it in only twelve minutes!"

In some families, breakfast and TV must wait until the child is totally ready to leave the house—washed, dressed, and packed. The breakfast, entertainment, and praise serve as reinforcers for the child's successful Start behavior.

What about fighting, teasing, whining, or other Stop behavior in the morning? Stop behavior should be counted as usual. If there is time for a rest period, don't hesitate to use one. If there is not enough time, consider using a BreakTime alternative. "Guys, that's 3. Bedtime is fifteen minutes earlier for both of you tonight. OK, let's get in the car."

Responsibility Training for Older Kids

For children nine years old and up (including high school age), you can still use the methods just described. But if you have the guts—and if you'd like to get out of an unwanted supervisory role faster—here's a version of natural consequences for you. This up-and-out program involves some drastic alterations in the morning routine, and these changes will often shock the kids into being much more responsible for themselves. But be forewarned: extreme self-restraint on the part of moms and dads is required.

Before explaining this new regime, we remind parents that—believe it or not—most kids want to go to school and would be embarrassed if they were late or didn't show up at all. Parents don't appreciate that their kids feel this way because the kids goof off in the morning instead of getting ready. But the kids dillydally precisely because their parents have habitually taken *all* the responsibility for them getting to school on time.

Now that way of thinking is going to change—in both children and parents. Here's how the new procedure works. You explain to the kids that from now on, it will be their responsibility—not yours—to get up and out in the morning. You will neither supervise them nor nag them. If you have been waking them up, you will wake them up only once from now on. A better system is to get an alarm clock or cell phone with an alarm function and show the child how to use it. Explain to the kids that if they go back to sleep after your one wake-up call or after the alarm goes off, you will not wake them again and they will definitely have a problem.

You make it clear to the kids that getting up, getting dressed, washing up, eating breakfast, and leaving on time will be their job—totally. If you wish, you can chart the kids on how well they do getting up and out, but other than casual conversation, you will not say anything to them.

Your children will not believe that you are serious, because they will find it completely incomprehensible that you would ever allow them to get to school late. (You may have trouble with that concept too!) So guess what? You are going to have to make believers out of them.

This new system relies on natural consequences. If the kids dillydally in the morning, they are going to run into trouble somewhere. The trouble may be with the other kids in the car pool, who are now afraid that they are going to be late because of your son or daughter. (Can you stand that?) Or the trouble may come from the child having to explain to a principal or teacher why he was

> **Quik Tip**
> Tell your older kids that from now on, getting up and out in the morning is going to be their responsibility—totally. You will neither supervise nor nag them. At first, your children will not believe you are serious, but they *will* believe you are serious after you've let them get burned a few times. What's your chief job in all this? It's keeping quiet.

late and has no parental note excusing him. Most kids don't want these kinds of problems, so we use the threat of these natural consequences to help shape them up.

Some parents can't stand this routine. It drives some grown-ups crazy to watch their kids fooling around when the bus or car-pool ride is coming in five minutes. These are the moments when extreme parental self-restraint is called for. You will want to talk, nag, argue, or scream. I've had to ask many parents to take their coffee, retire to the bedroom, and not watch the impending disaster. One mother told me, "If I'm going to have to keep quiet and not watch, I want a martini—not a cup of coffee!"

Breakfast is optional for these older children. You can put some food out if that was your usual routine before, but you can't remind the kids to eat it. It's better if the kids just get what they want for themselves. Children won't die from missing breakfast. When they leave, you say nothing about coats, hats, or gloves, unless there is danger of frostbite.

What you are doing with this new up-and-out arrangement is teaching the kids responsibility and invoking a sacred rule of psychology: sometimes the hard way is the best way to learn. The lessons sink in more when kids get burned a few times than when they simply hear a lecture. So you have to be willing to let the kids get burned. Don't even start this procedure unless you are convinced you are ready for the strain and—more important—that you can keep quiet.

It usually takes no more than five days for the child to shape up and successfully get up and out on his own. During that five-day period, your child will probably be late to school a few times and will feel embarrassed. He will have had the experience of suddenly realizing at seven fifty that he's not dressed and that Mom didn't remind him that his ride was coming at eight. He may have gotten to school and realized he forgot his math book because he was late leaving. He may also have blown up at his mother a few times (and been counted!) because she didn't provide any reminders or excuse notes.

Kids have four ways of getting to school: car pool, bus, walking, or riding bikes. When they can walk or bike to school, of course, this up-and-out program is the easiest. With car pools or bus, you can drive the kids if they don't make their connection. Don't rush, however; let them get to school late. Most kids will not get dependent on your driving, especially if they're tardy anyway. If you do have to drive the kids, don't lecture on the way.

These negative experiences have quite an impact on most kids. If the parents are consistent, don't talk, and let the kids get burned, the children will shape up in a few days. No "I told you so" comments are allowed. Then things will be much more peaceful at home in the morning and the kids will be much more responsible.

Some parents have used charting along with our natural consequences program. If you decide to do this, make sure you praise good performances ("It's so much easier with you getting yourself up in the morning!") and review the chart at least once a week. You can discuss the issue, listen, give brief suggestions, or make modifications at times other than when the kids are getting ready in the morning.

Facing Morning Routine Challenges

Before they've used this gutsy procedure, many parents think their kids will be indifferent. Moms and dads think their children really won't care whether or not they get to school on time. Part of the reason the grown-ups believe this is because the children have said so. Never believe a child who says "I don't care." He usually means the opposite.

If you are skeptical about this up-and-out procedure, consider trying this arrangement and see what happens. Most kids—not all, but most—will shape up. The kids will get up and out on their own. The most important rules are to keep quiet and be willing to let the children suffer the consequences—more than once, if necessary. You may want to let the school know what you're doing. Most teachers and principals will cooperate with you, especially if you explain your purpose and label the procedure "independence training."

What if you just don't think you can stand it? Remember that you have other Start behavior tools for establishing routines. Consider charting, perhaps with artificial reinforcers, and the use of a kitchen timer. Since these kids are older, you might also discuss your morning routines at a family meeting. (See chapter 22.) One way or another, though, it is absolutely critical for everyone to start the day on a positive note. Adults take bad memories from unsuccessful mornings to work with them, and kids can take those same lousy memories to school.

If you are successful using natural consequences, relax and enjoy your kids, another cup of coffee, and the peace and quiet. Good luck!

The Invisible Manager Inside Your Child's Head

We sometimes *underestimate* our children's brains. We often think we need to provide them with more prompting, supervision, and motivation than we really do. This is often true when it comes to the issue of elementary age kids getting up and out in the morning for school.

Prompting, for example: Did you know your child's brain has a memory part called the hippocampus that makes your child very aware of the fact that it's a school day? Supervision: There's a frontal cortex in there that knows how to carry out the steps required to get up, get dressed, eat, pack a school bag, and get out the door on time. Motivation: Your child's brain has an amygdala that provides emotional punch to the operation, as in extreme anxiety about being late to school or not showing up.

How much are you, the parent, really necessary for this early morning operation?

CHAPTER SUMMARY
Morning Routine

1. Out of bed
2. Bathroom, wash up, brush teeth
3. Get dressed
4. Breakfast
5. Leave on time with the right equipment

14
CLEANING UP AND CHORES

Tips for Getting Your Kids to Clean Up after Themselves

WHILE OUR RESEARCH OVER the years has indicated that whining is the most aggravating Stop behavior problem for parents of young children, kids not cleaning up after themselves has consistently won out as the most irritating Start behavior problem. Some kids leave their stuff strewn all over the house, but amazingly they also have enough left to mess up their entire bedroom. And other undone chores compete with messy houses and messy rooms in the battle to drive parents crazy.

Unfortunately for us, most kids are not naturally neat. Perhaps the picking up and chore genes are missing from their chromosomal makeup. Conclusion? Children need to be trained to pick up, clean their rooms, and do chores.

How can you do that? By this time you shouldn't have to be reminded that you won't get the kids to complete these unpleasant tasks by nagging or delivering the lecture, "The Seven Reasons Why It's Easier on Me for You to Have a Clean Room." Counting isn't so helpful either here, because it doesn't provide the long-term motivation needed to complete chores.

Instead, you have several options for your kids who are four, five, and older. Here are some good ones.

Strategies for Dealing with Messy Bedrooms

Your stomach churns with disgust when you view the destruction and chaos that is your daughter's bedroom. Things are thrown all over. You've forgotten what color the carpet was. The cat was last seen in there three weeks ago. Here a couple of simple routines.

Close the Door and Don't Look

Having a clean room is not a life-or-death matter. We know of no research indicating that kids who didn't keep their rooms neat grow up to be violent or more likely to divorce. Besides, whose room is it? You don't have to live in it, so why not just ask the child to keep the door closed so you don't have to deal with the aggravation?

Most parents don't like this idea, but before you dismiss the close-the-door-and-don't-look method, ask yourself one question: Do you have a child with behavioral or emotional problems, such as ADHD, learning disability, anxiety, or depression? If you have a handicapped child or one who's very difficult to begin with, why add another set of difficulties to your problems?

Imagine that your daughter hates school, hates homework, has no friends, feels lousy most of the time, and fights with her brother constantly. Should you also get after her about the stuff lying around on her bedroom floor? You need to straighten out your priorities, because you have bigger fish to fry. Option 1 sure beats yelling and nagging.

Option 1 is quite legitimate for some families, but there are two problems with this procedure: (1) most parents find the notion unacceptable, and (2) dirty dishes and dirty laundry can't be ignored.

If you don't want to use Option 1, more suggestions will follow in the next sections of this chapter. As for dirty dishes and dirty clothes, you can try almost any other Start behavior tactic. A timer, charting, or the 1-2-3 method (if the dishes or clothes can be picked up in less than two minutes) can be helpful. Remember to praise compliance from time to time with older kids and frequently with younger children.

Some parents whose kids are older simply tell them that any clothes that don't make it to the laundry or hamper don't get washed. Then the child has to wash them herself. Those are examples of natural consequences. The docking system can also be considered. You go and get the dirty clothes or dishes from the room, but you charge for your labor. You'll feel better about having to do the job. Make sure you keep your mouth shut about the whole operation and keep the fees reasonable.

The Weekly Cleanup Routine

Don't like Option 1? Option 2 is a favorite with many moms and dads. With the weekly cleanup routine, the kids have to clean their rooms only once a week, but according to your specifications. You might explain that the following chores have to be done: pick up toys, put clothes in hamper, make bed, maybe vacuum. A specific day and time, such as Saturday morning, is chosen, and the child is not allowed to go outside, play, or do anything else until his room is done and you've approved it.

Cleaning the room is a Start behavior, and you will be rewarding the child immediately after the room cleaning with both freedom and praise. If artificial reinforcers are necessary, these rewards will be tallied or recorded at checkout time, potentially with a chart.

Many parents have tried something like the weekly cleanup routine, but the grown-ups often ruin the whole procedure by getting into an argument with the child at checkout. Never argue about what needs to be done; make the specifications clear in the first place. For example:

"I'm done with my room. Can I go out now?"

"Your bed's not finished."

"Whaddaya mean? That's good enough."

(Dad turns to walk away.)

"What's the matter with it?"

"That's 1."

"Oh, for Pete's sake!" *(Goes to finish bed.)*
This dad had already explained that the bed had to be neatly made, so there was no need for further talk. His son starts testing, using the badgering tactic, and after ignoring the badgering once, Dad uses the 1-2-3 strategy. If the child winds up back in his room with a 3 count and a BreakTime, that's perfect! He'll have a few minutes to make his bed properly.

Tactics for Picking Up around the House

Let me make one thing perfectly clear: The close-the-door-and-don't-look method applies only to the kids' rooms. The scheme does not apply to the rest of your house! You shouldn't allow the children to leave your kitchen, family room, dining room, bathrooms, and hallways cluttered with their things. (As all parents know, kitchen counters and tables are such convenient dumping grounds.) You certainly can't close a door and not look when the entire house is involved. Here are some useful routines for common areas of the house.

Kitchen Timer and Docking System

These two Start behavior tactics can be very handy in getting the house picked up—especially when you can't avoid having to straighten up on the spur of the moment. When the job has to be done right away, the timer is helpful for picking up public areas such as family rooms and kitchens. If a surprise guest is coming over, you may not have much time to play around:

"Hey, kids. Mr. and Mrs. Johnson are coming over in forty-five minutes. I'll need all your stuff out of the kitchen by then. I'm setting the timer."

When using the timer like this, it's perfectly OK (and fun) to add an artificial reward if the room is done within a certain time. Or even an artificial punishment if it's not—they don't do it, they pay you. Just be sure not to use artificial rewards for everything you ask the kids to do. Your praise should be enough reward most of the time—and don't forget that part of a child's satisfaction when you praise him is knowing that he did something that made you happy.

The Garbage Bag Method

This procedure has been a favorite of parents for many years. The deal is this: you first encourage the children as much as possible not to leave their stuff lying around the house. You're not going to expect perfection. "Stuff" includes clothes, DVDs, books, papers, toys, Barbies, shoes, pens, comics, electronic games, videos, fossils, and so on.

Next, you tell the kids that at a certain time every day, their things have to be removed from the public areas of the house and returned to their bedrooms. Maybe you pick 8:00 p.m. as the cutoff time. You will pick up anything left out after eight and put it in a big garbage bag or some other container. The child will lose the right to use those items until 6:00 p.m. the following day. You can set the times however you want.

Some parents threaten to actually throw away the things they find that are not put away. There are two problems with this notion. First, if you do throw away some of your children's possessions, that's pretty harsh (but parents have done it!). After all, they're just kids and don't have an inherent desire to pick up after themselves. Second, it's likely you won't really throw the stuff away. You'll just go blustering around about that possibility and how unfair your life is. In this case, you are simply making a useless, empty threat, and the kids will catch on to you right away.

So imagine you're using the garbage bag routine and have picked 8:00 p.m. as the cutoff time. At 7:50 p.m. you remind seven-year-old Caitlin that her things need to be picked up. She doesn't respond because she

> **Quik Tip**
> Your kids do not have a right to mess up your entire house! Tell the children that by a certain time every day, anything of theirs that you find lying around will be confiscated and unavailable to them until a certain time the following day. Pick up the kids' things without grumbling or lecturing. You'll soon find that before the magic hour comes each day, they will be scurrying around to salvage their possessions.

doesn't really think you'll do anything about it. At 8:05 p.m., however, when you quietly begin walking around with a large plastic bag and have already claimed five of her prized possessions, Caitlin becomes a believer. She runs around frantically grabbing whatever of hers she can find before you get to it and yelling, "This is stupid! This isn't fair!"

You consider counting her screaming, but you don't. You put the bag away in your bedroom closet. The following night at seven fifty, when you say "Cleanup time!" Caitlin scurries around retrieving her things and then takes them to her bedroom. You say, "Good job, Caitlin—it looks real nice in here!" You are a model of restraint and a motivational wizard.

The 55-Gallon Drum

I cannot take credit for this next plan. A lady described it when I spoke with her on the phone many years ago. She told me that picking up around her house had never been a problem. This resourceful mother kept a 55-gallon metal drum in the garage, which was right next to her kitchen. Whenever she found anything of her children's that was out of place, she would simply put the items in the metal drum.

This procedure had become so routine with her four boys that whenever one of the kids couldn't find something of his, he would simply look in the drum. One day, for example, her second oldest came running into the kitchen and exclaimed, "Mom, I can't find my gym shoes. Are they in the drum?" "Yes," was his mother's reply, and the incident was over.

You say you don't happen to have a 55-gallon drum handy, or your kids couldn't reach in there if you did? A large box will do fine.

How to Handle Chores

By now you could probably write this section on chores yourself! We only need to make a few more points. First of all, praise your little ones (five and under) whenever they help out, but don't expect them to be able to remember or to sustain work projects for more than a few minutes. Second, when the kids are approximately seven and older, consider using the family meeting (see chapter 22) to discuss and divide up the jobs that regularly need to be done. This planning will help you avoid the curse of the spontaneous request, which we mentioned earlier.

Third, charting is an excellent tactic for chores. The chart serves as both a reminder of what needs to be done and a record of how well the task was accomplished. When charting chores, consider trying only natural reinforcers (praise, the chart itself, and job satisfaction) initially. See how far you get with naturals and only use artificial rewards (allowance, points, and so on) if you're not getting anywhere because the task is so obnoxious or foreign to your child.

Fourth, the docking system is also perfectly suited to chores. If the kids don't do what they're supposed to, you quietly do it for them and they pay you. The payment should not be accompanied by a parental lecture about responsibility. Also be forewarned that some kids will happily pay you for doing their jobs, and their chore-completion behavior will not improve. What do you do in this case? You can up the ante—they pay more for you to do the chore. Or you can just take the money and run. Consider this an introduction for your child to the workings of a service economy: you don't get free service; you pay for it. There's a lesson in that for your kids.

One final word about pets. Caring for an animal is obviously a chore. When they are overwhelmed with excitement about getting a cat or dog, most kids don't realize that eventually they'll have to regularly complete boring tasks, such as feeding, watering, cleaning up, and brushing. When it comes to pets, our Start behavior tactics are not all equally helpful. Praise, the use of a timer, and charting can all be useful, of course. The natural consequences tactic is inappropriate, however, because this method endangers the animal. Perhaps the best method for pets is the docking system, because you can care for the pet while your child is learning to be more responsible.

With regard to pets, however, the best advice for parents is this: don't get any animal that you don't want to take care of yourself.

Train Them Early!

Everyone, it seems, considers the word *chore* to be a dirty word. But surprisingly, there's one group of people who do not feel this way: toddlers and preschoolers. These little ones love to help sweep with a broom, scrub a toilet, vacuum, put stuff in the garbage, feed the dog, or even dust.

Why? Because at these early ages, kids' brains are programmed to want to do what the big people are doing. In a teen, the same motivation might prompt an interest in smoking or driving. But the preschoolers are passionate about their motivation to imitate adults—they want to do what you're doing, and they want to do it themselves. Even though the kids' efforts are often sloppy at these ages, we really need to encourage this early inspiration instead of killing it off by nagging them to clean their rooms.

So let the preschoolers help sloppily. Then give six-, seven-, and eight-year-olds more meaningful, self-esteem-building tasks, such as cooking for the family and shopping or doing homework and getting up and out for school completely on their own.

CHAPTER SUMMARY
Parents' Favorite Routines for Cleaning Up and Chores

For cleaning rooms:
The Weekly Cleanup Routine

For picking up around the house:
The Garbage Bag Method

For chores (except homework):
The Docking System

15
SURVIVING SUPPERTIME
What to Do When Your Kids Won't Eat

THEY SAY MEALTIMES ARE supposed to be a time for family togetherness and family bonding. Dinnertime is a time to open up, talk about your day, and enjoy everybody's company. Unfortunately, when you mix general childhood fidgetiness, a little sibling rivalry, a finicky vegetable-eater or two, and tired adults, you often have the recipe for an unpleasant occasion.

Picky Pete Who Would Not Eat

Here's a situation most parents have experienced at one time or another. It's suppertime at the Jenkins's house. Peter, however, is not a happy camper. He's picking unenthusiastically at his food while his sister, Alicia, happily chows down.

Mom: "Come on, Peter. Let's get going."
Peter: "I'm not hungry."
Dad: "What did you have to eat after school?"
Peter: "Not that much."

Dad: "Then how come you're not eating?"
Peter: "I am eating!"
Mom: "No you're not!"
Peter: "We never have anything I like."
(Silence. Frustrated parents look at each other and continue eating.)
Peter: "Why do I have to eat this stuff?"
Mom: "Because, you know, you want to grow up to be big and strong. You need energy."
Peter: "But I don't like any of it."
Mom: "OK, if you don't finish, there will be no dessert and nothing else to eat before bed. Do you understand?"
Alicia: "I like what we're having."
Peter: "Oh, shut up!"
Dad: "Peter, you've got five minutes to finish."
Peter: "Dog food's better than this junk!"
Dad: "Up to your room, right now, young man! That's no way to talk to anyone!"
(Peter stomps up to his room. Alicia takes another big bite.)

This scene is not a warm-and-friendly family interaction. This episode has all the elements for disaster: one picky eater, two fighting siblings, and two weary parents who are talking too much and asking silly questions. Here are several routines to help avoid this kind of trouble.

> **Quik Tip**
> Try this with your finicky eaters. Give the kids super-small portions and then set the timer for twenty minutes. If the children finish before the timer goes off, they get their dessert. You may not nag or prompt—the timer will do that for you.

Strategies for Mealtime

Small Portions and a Kitchen Timer
Do you have fussy eaters like Picky Pete? Get out a kitchen timer and set it for twenty minutes when you all sit down at the table. Tell the kids they have to finish their dinner in that time. If they

do finish the meal in twenty minutes, they get their dessert. You're not allowed to prompt anyone to eat; that's what the timer is for.

When you start the kitchen timer method, initially give your hard-to-please children very small portions of foods they don't like. Even ridiculously small, if necessary, such as three peas, a tablespoon of scalloped potatoes, and two bites of pork chop. Research shows that children who are exposed to new foods but not forced to eat them will often come around and start to enjoy some of the more exotic possibilities. That result is a lot healthier for them in the long run.

If the kids goof around or fight at the dinner table, they get counted. If anyone hits a count of 3, he is timed out for five minutes while the twenty minutes on the timer keep on ticking. You may not make comments such as, "Come on now, don't forget the timer's ticking," or "Quit that goofing around and get down to eating, young man!" You are probably also aware by now that you should not count the kids for not eating. Eating is a Start behavior, not a Stop behavior. What will help prompt the children to wolf down the chow? The timer: tick, tick, tick. You can praise the kids when they do eat.

What if the timer rings and there is still food on the plates? No dessert—at least yet. The plate goes into the kitchen and onto the counter. Cover the leftovers with plastic wrap. After a half hour has expired, the children have the right to finish the meal if they wish. The food can be quickly nuked in the microwave if necessary. If the children don't ever eat the rest of their meal, that's fine—but still no dessert. Some parents throw the rest of the child's dinner down the disposal when the timer hits twenty minutes, but this procedure seems a little extreme.

Stay on your toes when a hungry little tot who didn't finish her dinner puts the hit on you later for some treats.

ROUND ONE

"I'm ready for my ice cream now."

"You'll have to finish your dinner first, honey."

"It's all cold."

"We'll just heat it in the microwave for a few seconds, and it'll be good as new."

"I didn't like it anyway. I just want a little ice cream."

"Now you know the rules, dear. You have to finish what's on your plate first. Remember, we didn't give you that much in the first place."

"I never get anything!"

"What are you talking about—you never get anything? That's enough of that! Either finish your dinner or stop bugging me!"

"I hate you!"

This interaction was an unfortunate waste of time and also very hard on this relationship.

ROUND TWO

The conversation should have gone like this:

"I'm ready for my ice cream now."

"You'll have to finish your dinner first, honey."

"It's all cold."

"We'll just heat it in the microwave for a few seconds, and it'll be good as new."

"I didn't like it anyway. I want just a little ice cream."

"That's 1."

"Then I'll go to bed starving!" *(Walks away)*

Mom did much better. There were no Little Adult explanations, and Mother ignored her daughter's martyrdom.

The Three-Out-of-Four Rule

Let's return to the case of Picky Pete. Imagine that Peter's parents sit down, review the mealtime situation, and come up with a new plan. Mom and Dad explain the new deal to their son. If Peter eats three out of four items on his plate, the boy can have his dessert. The serving sizes will be smaller, and Peter has to at least taste the one thing he doesn't choose to eat.

The first meal under the new regime goes well. Even though they are a bit nervous, both parents avoid any anxious prompting. Peter finishes his smaller portions of pork, mashed potatoes, and peas. After tasting it, he forgoes the salad. He gets ice cream for dessert.

After the mealtime overhaul, the first week passes without any unpleasant incidents. Peter and his parents actually enjoy one another's company. The dinner table conversation is spirited and friendly.

"Pete, how was that movie you saw with your friend?"

"Oh, cool! You guys gotta see it!"

"You really think we'd like it at our advanced ages?"

"Oh, yeah! Let's go—I'll go see it again."

"Well, if your mother's willing, it might be possible."

"Mom, you gotta go. It's so neat! There's this one part where…"

That's the way meals should be. But what if Peter and Alicia start fighting? They will both be counted. In our original scene, it would go something like this:

Peter: "But I don't like any of it."

Mom: "OK, if you don't finish, there will be no dessert and nothing else to eat before bed. Do you understand?"

Alicia: "I like what we're having."

Peter: "Oh, shut up!"

Mom: "That's 1 for each of you."

Some of you may wonder why Alicia should be counted. All she did was say, "I like what we're having." Can you guess the answer? It was all in her rose-colored but competitive timing.

> **Key Concept**
> Who says you have to eat dinner together every single night of the year? Consider having some special nights where each person eats wherever she wishes. Or—better yet—have some nights when one parent takes one child out to eat. It's different and it's fun!

The Divide-and-Conquer Routine

Many parents seem to feel that there is a federal law dictating that every family eat supper together every night of the year. This is the time, the experts claim, for "family togetherness" and for each person to "share his or her day" with everyone else. Sometimes, however, dinner becomes a time for people to share their hostility toward everyone else. Tempers as well as appetites can be lost.

What can a parent do to improve this situation? One solution, obviously, is to not eat together every night. Though some people consider this sacrilegious, it sure beats fighting all the time. Now you only have to fight every other night!

Seriously, sometimes you might consider feeding the kids first or occasionally letting them eat in front of the TV. Or, now and then, let the kids eat wherever they want to, as long as they bring back their dishes. Then Mom and Dad can eat in the kitchen or have a peaceful dinner together later, or if you're a single parent, you might want a little time to yourself once in a while.

Another idea is for each parent to periodically take one child out to dinner as a kind of special occasion. Once a week isn't a bad idea at all. This one-parent, one-child setup is one that the kids love. It's also one where sibling rivalry is not possible, so the parent is much more relaxed and able to enjoy himself.

Think about suppertime. Eating supper should be a pleasant experience. In fact, for most children, eating is a natural and enjoyable activity that doesn't require much parental intervention. With a little planning you can enjoy your evenings a lot more.

Brains Like Good Food and Good Company

Everybody's brain—yours and your child's—needs good food on a regular basis. But it's also important for good neurological development that breakfast, lunch, and suppertime be free from anxiety and hassle. Parental comments such as "Why aren't you eating?" or "We'll just sit here until you finish those peas!" seriously interfere with both the intake and the processing of the critical nutrition your child's brain needs.

The ideal is a mealtime totally free of parental supervision but full of people enjoying one another's company. Your child's brain, for the most part, already knows how to eat. Don't get in the way of that natural process.

CHAPTER SUMMARY
Possible Suppertime Routines

1. Small portions and a kitchen timer
2. The Three-Out-of-Four Rule
3. The Divide-and-Conquer Routine

16
TACKLING THE HOMEWORK PROBLEM

What to Do When Schoolwork Is Taking Over Your Family

HOMEWORK CIVIL WARS MAKE school nights miserable for the whole family. Schoolwork battles can go on for two, three, or four hours a night. People begin to dread the evening, relationships become strained, and the child in question learns to hate schoolwork more and more. There's Brother sitting at the kitchen table after dinner staring out the window with a sour look on his face. The boy's sister, who completed her homework years ago, sits in the other room, smugly watching TV. Mom and Dad check in the kitchen every five or ten minutes to badger the distinguished academic. Overall, a rotten end to the day.

How can you make homework time tolerable and efficient?

Spontaneous Requests Strictly Forbidden!

First of all, the worst mistake you can make is to ask your child—just when you happen to think about it—if he has homework. This is an example of a spontaneous request, and your question is sure to provoke hostility. Homework should be a daily routine, done at the same time and in the same place as much as possible.

One of the best ways of setting up a good routine is to have the child come home, get a snack, goof around for thirty to forty-five minutes, and then sit down in a quiet spot and try to finish his schoolwork before dinner. Then the whole evening is free—and it will be free of homework hassles for you! For many but not all children, afternoon is preferable to evening for homework because the child has more energy.

Don't let your young student do academic work with the TV on. The television is always out to get your attention. Believe it or not, music from a CD or iPod may be fine. For many children and teens, music can provide consistent background noise that blocks out other household distractions.

Helpful Homework Strategies

Natural Consequences

If you are going through the first experiences of your child having trouble with homework, consider trying the natural consequences approach first. That means you do nothing. Keep quiet and see if the child and the teacher can work things out. So many parents get anxious way too soon about their children's schoolwork, with the result that the grown-up prematurely takes charge of the job and doesn't give the child a chance to learn—and exercise—true responsibility.

Let your daughter, for example, explain to *her* teacher why *her* work was not completed. And when your daughter later complains to you about how irritated her teacher was with her for not turning in her homework, instead of saying, "I told you so," say, "That must have been embarrassing for you, but I'm sure you'll do better." If this approach doesn't seem to be working after a few weeks, then switch to some of the other alternatives described in this chapter.

You obviously can't rely on natural consequences to solve the behavior, if you have been having homework problems for years and years. With chronic problems, you will need to take a closer look at why your child is having such a hard time. Children with learning disabilities and attention-deficit problems, for instance, not only need a well-thought-out daily homework routine but may also benefit from tutoring, treatment, or other academic accommodations.

Assignment Sheets

Assignment sheets or assignment notebooks can be extremely helpful for kids who have homework troubles. Assignment notebooks tell you exactly what work is due for each subject, which—among other benefits—helps prevent lying about homework. Many schools now have Internet-based homework hotlines where forgetful but fortunate kids can log on after hours to find out what their assignments are.

Part of the idea of the assignment sheet, of course, is that after the child does the work, the parents can check it against the list of items to be done. If this is the procedure you are considering, you should routinely include our next two homework procedures: the PNP Method and the Rough Checkout.

The PNP Method

Suppose your daughter has just completed her midweek spelling pretest. There are ten words on the list, and she spelled nine correctly and misspelled one. When she brings you her paper, your first job, naturally, is to point out the word she spelled wrong. Right?

Wrong! PNP stands for "Positive-Negative-Positive." Whenever a child brings any piece of schoolwork to you, the first thing out of your mouth must be something positive—some compliment. You might, for instance, praise the child for remembering to show you her work. After saying something nice about the child's effort, you may then make a negative comment, if it's absolutely necessary. Finally, you should conclude your insightful remarks with another piece of positive feedback. So the procedure is Positive-Negative (if necessary)-Positive.

The Rough Checkout

Our next idea, the Rough Checkout, will also help to make your evenings a lot more pleasant. The Rough Checkout notion is based on the fact that eight in the evening is no time to expect scholastic perfection. You have worked all day, and your child has put in about the equivalent of a day on a full-time job—before she even started her homework!

Unless there is some major indication to the contrary, if your daughter's schoolwork is anywhere near 80 percent neat, correct, and thorough, consider the job done. Let your child and teacher continue worrying about the assignment tomorrow.

This advice is doubly true for ADHD or LD children who are already having a tough enough time with school. You can also adjust your Rough Checkout criteria to your child's overall achievement level. If, for example, your child is generally an excellent student (A-B average), you might consider raising the required neat, correct, and thorough percentage to 90 or more.

I learned this advice the hard way. A mother once came into my office reporting that her twelve-year-old son was getting more depressed, more irritable, and more distant from everyone in the family. It turned out that homework was a major problem for this boy every night. The boy would finish his assignments and bring them to his father for checkout. That was the good news. The bad news was that if the work was not absolutely perfect, Dad would tear it up and make his son start over!

So, if your child's work is for the most part neat, correct, and complete—but not perfect—consider the PNP procedure. Don't tell the child that his schoolwork is superb, because it's not. Just say that the work is good and praise some specific parts of what he has done. Perfectionist parents who squirm at this suggestion need to stay in touch with the emotional realities of childhood and the value of holding their children to realistic expectations.

Charting for Homework

A daily charting system can be a godsend in improving academic work and decreasing homework hostilities. This is especially true when charting is combined with the Rough Checkout and Positive-Negative-Positive methods, and when spur-of-the-moment homework requests are avoided.

Since older kids are usually the ones who have trouble with homework, a five-point scale can be used on the chart instead of stickers. Five is the highest mark and one is the lowest mark. A child can earn one point for each of the following things:

> **Quik Tip**
> The first thing out of your mouth when your child shows you her homework must be something positive—even if it's just that she brought her work to you. And remember: 8:00 p.m. is no time to expect academic perfection!

Neat:	1 point
Correct:	1 point
Thorough:	1 point
No complaining:	1 point
Starting on your own at the right time without being reminded:	1 point
TOTAL POSSIBLE SCORE:	5 points

Kids can get each of the first three points by doing better than whatever approximate percentage of neatness, correctness, and completeness you have required according to your Rough Checkout rules. The no-complaining point is earned if the child doesn't whine or grouse about having to do his schoolwork.

The last point is the crucial one. We sometimes call the fifth point the "Magic Point," because if you can get a child to start

> **Quik Tip**
> When charting homework performance using our five-point system, the fifth point is the Magic Point. A child earns the fifth point for starting his schoolwork at the right time without being reminded. That's half the battle!

his work on his own, in a timely fashion and without being reminded, the battle is more than half won! You can also set up friendly incentive games with this last Magic Point. For example, three days in a row of starting on your own at the proper time earns a bonus point. Or starting more than fifteen minutes early and finishing in a reasonable amount of time earns two bonus points.

Remember that for many kids with academic handicaps, you may have to use artificial reinforcers to help motivate the child over the homework hurdle. Your successful young scholar, for example, might earn a special outing with you, a special meal, part of his allowance early, or time on a new game for posting a certain number of points during the week. Different rewards may require different numbers of points. Check back to our list of possible rewards in chapter 12.

Also, don't forget that kitchen timer when dealing with homework. One helpful tactic is to use the device to help break up the work into smaller, manageable fifteen-to-twenty-minute pieces. A timer also helps keep kids on task. If your child complains that the timer's ticking bothers him, use a sand hourglass, computer, or LCD device.

Getting homework time down to a manageable routine can do wonders for your kids as well as for you. Homework won't necessarily become fun, but it should not be a daily battle between you and your child. If you have tried the tactics suggested here for four to six weeks and you still feel that things are not going well enough, it may be time for a professional evaluation or an evaluation by the school. Vision and hearing difficulties, specific learning disabilities, attention deficits, and a host of other problems can make schoolwork way too hard for some kids. A diagnostic workup is especially indicated when a child has academic trouble at school and is also struggling to complete schoolwork at home.

Human Brains Carry Out Plans

As your child gets older, his or her ability to carry out a plan will get better and better. To carry out a plan, you need to remember what to do (what the plan is), recall the steps involved, and then carry out those steps without getting distracted.

As kids' brains mature, they can implement plans that are longer and longer as well as more and more complex. It's fun to watch this development and maturation! A six-year-old, for example, can do about ten

EXECUTIVE FUNCTIONING:
- 7 YRS 20 MINUTES
- 8 YRS 30 MINUTES
- 9 YRS 40 MINUTES

minutes of unsupervised work that is not especially fun. For a typically developing youngster, the duration of their capacity for independent work will increase by about ten minutes per year.

CHAPTER SUMMARY
Homework Helpers

1. No spontaneous requests!
2. Natural consequences
3. The Positive-Negative-Positive (PNP) Method
4. The Rough Checkout
5. Charting

Use the same tactics for practicing obnoxious musical instruments!

17

GOING TO BED—AND STAYING THERE!

How to Handle the Nightmare of Bedtime

FOR MANY FAMILIES, PUTTING the kids to bed is a daily nightmare. Although bedtime may technically be nine, at ten thirty the children are still wandering around the house, asking for drinks, telling you they heard a noise outside, or going to the bathroom for the twentieth time. This "routine" may be accompanied by a good deal of arguing, which only ensures that everyone will stay awake to watch the late movie together.

With a little thought, this bad end to your evenings can be eliminated. Your workdays are long enough as it is. Many of our Start behavior tactics can be used for bedtime. Put these strategies together, and you have some real and wonderfully helpful routines for managing going to bed, staying in bed, and nighttime waking. No parental wishful thinking allowed!

The Basic Bedtime Method

Before you do anything else, set a bedtime for the kids and stick to it. The bedtime may vary, of course, depending on whether it's a school night or a weekend, school year or summertime. But exceptions to the rule should be rare. Otherwise, bedtime is open to negotiation every night, and then to testing and manipulation.

Let's say you have a nine-year-old daughter, and you decide that nine will be the time for her to go to bed on a school night. The Basic Bedtime Method goes like this. At eight thirty you set a timer for thirty minutes and tell the child that it's time to get ready for bed. This means that your daughter must do everything required to prepare for bed (bathroom, teeth, pajamas, and so on)—on her own—and then report to you. Make the preparation routine perfectly clear. If your child is only two or three or four, you'll have to help her get ready, but the same rewards and consequences will apply.

When the child has completed all the necessary tasks, she reports to you. If she accomplished everything she had to, praise her for her efforts. Now comes the reward. Whatever time is left between eight thirty and nine is time for just the two of you. You might read a story or simply sit and talk. Kids love this kind of one-on-one time with a parent. Stay in the bedroom and don't do anything super exciting.

This special time serves three purposes. First, it is an immediate reinforcer for the child independently getting ready for bed. Second, the remaining minutes until nine are a nice time together. And finally, these moments with you help the kids relax and get in the mood—physically and mentally—for going to sleep.

If you have trouble coming up with an inventory of all that needs to be done for the kids to get ready for bed, just think of all the things the children usually tell you they haven't done after they are in bed, and you'll have the list right away:

> **Quik Tip**
> The Basic Bedtime Method will save you lots of aggravation in the evenings. The first requirement is that you pick a bedtime—and stick to it! Bedtime cannot be renegotiated every night.

"I'm hungry and I need a drink."
"I'm scared."
"I have to go to the bathroom."
"These pajamas itch."
"There's a burglar in the basement."

And so on, and so on. Every item on the list should be addressed as well as possible before your child gets into bed. One caution here. Don't lie down on the bed. There seems to be a biological law that says: If you are over twenty-five years of age, and it's past eight in the evening, and you spend more than three minutes in a horizontal position, you'll be out like a light. And the kids will love it! They'll enjoy the comfort and novelty of having you sleeping next to them, but they will also quickly get dependent on this arrangement and start expecting—or demanding—your presence every night.

And now, the grand finale. When nine rolls around, tuck the child in, kiss her good night, and leave the room. You have just had a nice time with your child, and your parenting job is done for the day.

Right? Perhaps not. At this point some parents say, "How naive you are. When I leave she's right behind me!" or "If I go down to the kitchen, she's sure to show up in less than three minutes." So what if your daughter won't stay in bed after nine?

Getting Out of Bed

Some kids just can't seem to stay in bed after you tuck them in. While you try to go about your business, they are always coming up with some new reason for getting out of bed. Why? Usually it's because the children are (1) scared, (2) bored, or (3) both.

When my son was eighteen months old, he climbed out of his crib for the first time. My wife and I were sitting in the living room of our two-flat, relaxing and thinking the day was over, when in walked this cute little kid, grinning from ear to ear, proud as punch that he had single-handedly escaped from his crib for the first time in his life. As young parents, we interpreted this event as the end of the known world. We had visions of our little guy getting up at three in the morning, calling his friends on the phone, roasting marshmallows on the gas stove, or worse.

In desperation—and forgetting temporarily that I was supposed to be a clinical child psychologist—I found some scrap lumber and bailing twine and built up the sides of his crib about a foot higher all the way around. The contraption worked for two nights.

On the third night our boy figured out a way to scale even these new heights and once again escape. So we had to come up with a new plan. Trying to reason with an eighteen-month-old would have been useless. Not only that, but now our son considered getting out of his crib an exciting challenge. So my wife and I decided that our only choice was to train him to remain in bed—or at least in his bedroom.

We put a chair in the door to his room, and after all the bedtime prep was done, one of us (we took turns) just sat in the chair, facing into the hallway. We left the side of his crib down, because putting it up was now useless, and we turned on a floor fan for background noise. We said nothing after bedtime. If our son got out of bed, we put him back. After awhile we'd give up on putting him back in bed, and he'd just fall asleep on the floor. Then we'd cover him and leave, because if we tried to pick him up, he'd wake up.

After a week or two, he started staying in his bed and going to sleep with no fuss. What a relief! He found our presence in the doorway comforting, even though we weren't talking. In another week or so, we no longer had to sit in there. A couple of months later, our little guy graduated to a junior bed.

The strategy for handling kids getting out of bed is based on a basic psychological principle: *if a child gets out of bed after bedtime, the longer he stays up, the more reinforcement he gets for this behavior.* And the more he will want to keep getting out of bed in the future. The essential conclusion, therefore, is that you have to "cut him off at the pass"— the doorway to the room. This tactic is no fun for Mom or Dad, but bedtime is not the time for wishful thinking. Bedtime is also not the time for ridiculous conversations with little kids about why they should stay in bed.

If you have a child who is older than five or six, you might be able to use charting to encourage him or her to stay in bed. If you are using charting with bedtime, however, you cannot tell the child right away how he did, because if he does really well, he won't be awake. Therefore, there will be a long delay—until the next morning—before he finds out how you rated him. But charting can still work, so keep it in mind.

> **Caution**
> Never forget one very important fact: if a child won't stay in bed at bedtime, the longer he is up and the farther he gets from his bedroom, the more reinforcement he will get from that activity. Your job? Cut him off at the pass.

Nighttime Waking

Some kids wake up during the night, make a little noise, and go right back to sleep. No problem! Other children may go through stages where they present themselves at your bedside in the middle of the night with a vague request for assistance. This can sometimes happen as many as a dozen or more times per night. Big problem!

Nighttime problems are among the hardest to handle, because in the middle of the night most parents aren't quite in their right minds—and neither are their kids. It can also be very aggravating to be awakened from a sound sleep, making it more difficult for you to respond appropriately.

When our daughter was seven, she went through a phase in which she would appear at our bedside in the middle of the night. When we would ask what the problem was, she would say something nonsensical, such as "The elephant ran away." Of course, at 2:00 a.m. you're not thinking clearly either, so we would respond with something equally ridiculous, such as "Well, where did he go?" These strange episodes went on for several months until we worked out the nighttime waking procedure that I'm about to describe.

Following are a number of steps that have

proved to be effective in responding to nighttime episodes. When these steps are carried out consistently and calmly, most kids will get back to sleeping through the night in a few weeks. Remember: if ever there was a time for our No Talking and No Emotion Rules, it's in the middle of the night!

Steps for Dealing with Nighttime Waking

1. **Accept some waking as normal.** Treat periodic nighttime waking as a temporary stage. This way of thinking will help you be less upset. Of course, if the problem has been going on for the last four years, it's not a temporary stage and you should talk to your pediatrician about the problem.
2. **Don't go to the child's room unless you must.** When do you have to go to the child's room during the night? If she is really upset or won't quiet down, you'd better check things out. On the other hand, many kids will make some noise, fuss for a while, and then go back to sleep. Give them a chance to do so.
3. **No talking and no emotion.** These calming rules apply doubly for nighttime incidents, because talking and emotion—especially anger—wake everyone up. Have you ever tried to sleep when you're furious? You can't. In the middle of the night, even asking a child what's wrong is usually pointless, because the child is groggy and can't tell you much that's useful.
4. **Assume the child has to go to the bathroom.** Your son appears at your bedside at 2:30 a.m., mumbling incoherently. Somebody is probably going to have to get up. This is an interesting situation, one in which certain people could win Academy Awards for sleeping performances. Dad's snoring deepens and the covers go over his head. Even though they don't or can't say it, many kids are awakened by the need to go to the bathroom. But they're so groggy they can't verbalize the physical sensation. So try steering or carrying them to the toilet and see what happens.

5. **Be gentle and quiet.** Handle and guide children softly as you stagger through the dark. Don't push them around, even though you may be irritated. You want them to remain sleepy.
6. **No lights!** Lights wake up parents and children very quickly, which then makes it hard to go back to sleep. Your eyes should be dark-adapted in the middle of the night, so move around as best you can in the dark.
7. **Don't let the child sleep with you regularly.** Sleeping together can become a habit that's hard to break later on. Unfortunately, letting the child crawl in bed with you is the easiest way to quiet him down immediately. In addition, staying in bed certainly is tempting, but you will pay for these moments of weakness in two ways. First, you will pay right away if the child really has to go to the bathroom, because he will remain squirmy. Second, you will pay later on when you cannot get the child to return to his room without having a tantrum.

One exception to this rule is this: if there's a terrible storm going on outside, complete with thunder and lightning, it can be beneficial to let the kids sleep on the floor next to your bed with sleeping bags and pillows, because they'll appreciate the psychological comfort. We had this deal with our kids when they were little. During any stormy night, within forty-five seconds of the first thunderous bang outside, our bedroom door would open and two small forms would appear. Each had a sleeping bag in one hand and a pillow in the other. It was cute. Without saying a word, the kids would plop down on the floor and immediately go back to sleep, suddenly oblivious to the storm. That's what parents are for.

Real-Life Bedtime Stories

Now, using our seven nighttime steps, let's see if we can persuade a few kids to go back to bed—and back to sleep.

- **Josh, age nine.** Josh has been sleeping regularly through the night. Tuesday night, however, he watched a scary movie on TV. At 2:45 a.m. you hear a few short, anxious, and disconnected sentences. You wait for a few minutes to see if he'll awaken or get up, but you don't go to his room. After a few minutes he goes back to sleep and is peaceful for the rest of the night.
- **Rachel, age six.** Rachel has been restless in bed for a few consecutive nights, but she hasn't gotten up yet. On Thursday night, however, she appears at your bedside, shakes your arm, and says she's scared. You say nothing, get up, put your arm gently around her shoulder, and steer her to the bathroom. She sits on the toilet for a while with no lights on. Rachel does have to go to the bathroom. When she's finished, you guide your daughter gently back to bed, tuck her in, and give her a kiss. You wait for a second by her door, see that she's falling asleep, and after she's quiet for a few minutes, you go back to bed.
- **Jim, age four.** Jim has been getting up several times a night. He won't go back to bed by himself and starts making a fuss if you tell him to. You can't tell if he's frightened or if it's something else. If you take him to his room, he cries or starts yelling when you try to leave. He says he wants to sleep with you. You know he's not sick—he just had a physical.

This situation is more difficult, obviously, than the first two examples. You don't want Jim to wake everyone in the house, but you don't like the idea of giving in to his testing either. What should you do?

When Jim appears at your bedside, you escort him to the bathroom first—no lights, no talking. He does need to urinate. Then you take him back to his room, put him in bed, and tuck him in. You know he'll probably cry if you try to leave, so before he has a chance to even get upset, get a chair, park yourself by the bed, and wait until he goes back to sleep. If you've done the main things right—such as no lights and no arguing—your son should still be somewhat sleepy. Though this routine is not fun, you soon find that the strategy is working. Jim is going right back to sleep.

With some kids this procedure must be repeated several times a night for several weeks before the child starts sleeping through, so brace yourself. Of all the families I've seen in my practice, the record for the most times getting up in one night is seventeen! This case involved a three-year-old girl, and we got her to sleep through the night in two months.

If you think you'll have to sit by the bed after tucking your child back in during the night, get your chair ready beforehand. Then, after a week or so of using this procedure, gradually start positioning the chair farther from the bed.

All Brains Need Lots of Sleep

Brains need a lot of sleep at night in order to be able to do their jobs during the day. That means your child's brain *and* your brain. That's why having a good nightly bedtime routine is so important.

Some parents spend two to three hours every night getting the kids to bed. That's bad, because it often means one and a half to two and a half hours of lost sleep—for everyone.

Scientists know very well what sleep deprivation does to the brains of children and adults. Sleep deprivation makes people crabby. Sleep deprivation makes it hard for kids to concentrate in school. And sleep deprivation makes moms and dads less patient, less affectionate, and less satisfied with themselves as parents. Use *1-2-3 Magic* to maximize everyone's natural sleep potential.

Now let's take a look at **Real-Life Story 3**. In *The Case of Bedlam at Bedtime*, you'll meet a little girl who was driving her parents crazy by not staying in bed. You'll also see how the parents solve the problem!

Real-Life Story 3

BEDTIME

As you are learning in *1-2-3 Magic*, a big part of Parenting Job 2, encouraging good behavior, is establishing reasonable and consistent routines. Kids do much better when the things you want them to accomplish—like eating supper and doing homework—are carried out each day at the same time and pretty much in the same way.

One of the most critical daily routines is getting the kids to bed—and getting them to stay there. Mess up this job and everyone will pay dearly, not only in the evening but the next day as well. That's what happened to us. We had to learn the hard way how to do bedtime with our young daughter, but what a relief once we figured it out!

Here's our story...

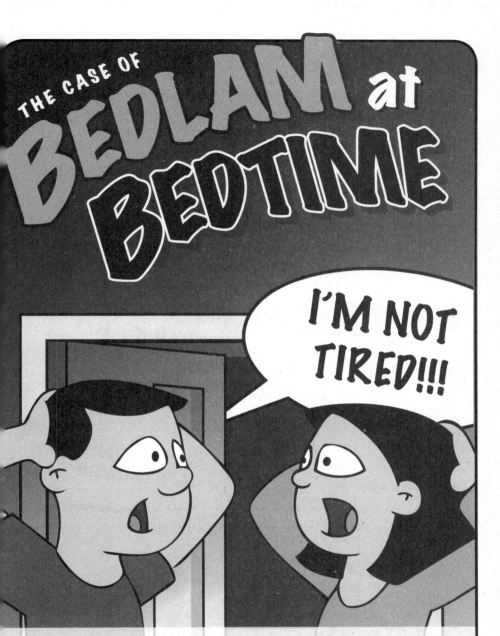

I was dragging around the whole day because I was so tired. My wife was having trouble at work because she was so tired. We were constantly crabby with each other, and we dreaded the evening. Why? Our daughter, Lucy, was cute as a button, but...

Obviously, this nighttime routine was one that we couldn't keep up for much longer. The funny thing was that we already had *1-2-3 Magic*, and we had been successfully using counting during the day with our daughter. But we didn't see how counting would help us with our little girl's refusing to stay in bed.

Guess what? Counting is *not* supposed to be used for this problem. Counting is more for controlling obnoxious behavior. Going to bed and staying there is basically a positive behavior that has to be encouraged with other tactics. Where would we find those strategies?

We had to finish reading *1-2-3 Magic*! We had been so delighted with the results of counting that we hadn't gone any further. There was a separate chapter called "Going to Bed—and Staying There!" There we learned the Basic Bedtime Method. First we had to pick a bedtime and stick with it. Then, a half hour before bedtime, we would inform Lucy that it was time to get ready for bed. She had to do everything to get ready and then check in with one of us. However much time was left in the half hour was story time or just one-on-one talking time. Then it would be lights-out.

What about her getting up all the time? Some kids keep getting up because they don't want the fun of the day to end. Others get up because they're scared. The "cut them off at the pass" procedure would take care of either possibility.

18
MANAGING YOUR EXPECTATIONS

What You Can Expect from Your Child, and When

AT THIS POINT WE'VE covered both Stop and Start behavior, but there is another underlying issue. When can you realistically expect (at what ages?) kids to potty train, clean their rooms, sit still, or finish their dinner? Lots and lots of parent-child conflict is caused not by kids misbehaving, but by parents not knowing exactly when they can expect what from their children. In other words, we parents often get impatient and expect too much too soon. When erroneous expectations are operating in a parent's brain, trouble follows.

Your kids are little. Both their bodies *and* their brains are still growing. No matter what your child is doing, his brain is working to create tons of new learning pathways and processing three times harder than an adult's. Ages birth to five are the times when the greatest amount of new learning and brain connecting takes place.

So it's important to be realistic and not set yourself and your kids up for conflict. The following is a list of our "Dirty Dozen"[1]—the twelve mistaken parental expectations that cause the most trouble. Be fair to yourself and your kids by memorizing these developmental milestones. There are plenty more. Two-year-olds don't read novels!

A Breakdown of the Dirty Dozen

1. Tantrums

Erroneous Expectation: Parents see kids' tantrums as unjustified, unnecessary, mean, exaggerated, and a sure sign of mental disorder.

The Reality: About 20 percent of two- to three-year-olds have daily tantrums, and meltdowns are equally common in boys and girls. Tantrums occur frequently in normal children aged about eighteen months through five years. Meltdowns are one way kids express their frustration with not getting what they want or with being told to do something they don't want to do. Kids are more prone to meltdowns when frustrated, tired, or sick.

What to Do: If your child has made a request for an item or an activity, be aware that you may soon be dealing with a tantrum. Give them what they want if you can, but if you can't, finalize your veto quickly and *stop talking*! Talking to a tantruming child is like pouring gasoline on a fire. If the child is safe, let the meltdown take its course and do not interact. Be gentle, forget the episode, and go on with your life!

2. They don't listen!

Erroneous Expectation: Parents expect kids to listen and respond the first time a parent makes a request.

---

1. *The Dirty Dozen: Faulty Parental Expectations* was coauthored by Dr. Sarah Levin Allen, Pediatric Neuropsychologist, Philadelphia, PA.

The Reality: Kids of all ages have trouble hearing and reacting to parental requests. Their minds are legitimately busy with other things. The younger kids are, the more difficulty they have tuning out the other things in their head and focusing on your agenda!

What to Do: Parents make two kinds of requests of their children—for Stop behavior and for Start behavior. Use your Start behavior tactics to set up routines. These strategies help stop the noise inside kids' heads and help them to begin the requested behavior. Stop behavior also requires a brain rebooting of sorts. For obnoxious behavior, 1-2-3 Magic suggests counting.

3. Sibling rivalry

Erroneous Expectation: Parents expect children to get along at all times without adult intervention.

The Reality: All siblings fight. Siblings three through seven years old fight about three to four times per hour. Younger kids can fight up to six times per hour—once every ten minutes. Ten- to fifteen-year-olds have the highest rate of sibling rivalry. More than 75 percent of children have had physical fights with their siblings. Boys tend to fight more physically, girls more emotionally.

What to Do: Whenever possible, don't get involved, unless there is risk of physical or emotional damage. If things are getting out of hand, use the 1-2-3 Magic strategy of counting both children. (It takes two to fight.) To help prevent sibling conflicts, try to ensure that children get approximately equal time with each parent by themselves.

4. Leaving anywhere!

Erroneous Expectation: Parents expect their children to be able to move—easily, quickly, and when asked the first time—from one activity or location to another.

The Reality: When they are doing something fun, *all* children have significant trouble switching to a new activity. Two- and three-year-olds are notoriously bad at changing places! Children must first stop the fun thing they are doing, then shift their attention to where they're going, then control their disappointment and move. Children's brains are working on these transition skills from birth all the way through the early twenties.

What to Do: Be prepared for resistance! Transitions are hard for your kids. Use sequential warnings and your 1-2-3 Magic timer. Give your child a two-minute, a one-minute, and then a thirty-second warning that it is time to stop a task or time to leave. If warnings do not help, stop talking and simply escort or carry the child to the next place or activity (and reread the first section on Tantrums!).

5. Potty training

Erroneous Expectation: Parents expect their children to be capable of peeing and pooping on the toilet at two years of age.

The Reality: The percentage of two-year-olds who have been successfully potty trained is about four percent. Only 60 percent of children have achieved mastery of the toilet by thirty-six months. Fifty-two percent of children are dry during the day at age three, and 93 percent are dry at the age of four. The average age for being dry at night is about four years. Pooping success tends to come after peeing success. In general, boys potty train later than girls, and daytime dryness almost always comes before nighttime dryness.

What to Do: Look for readiness signs in your child. Signs for potty readiness include interest in the toilet, randomly peeing in the toilet, being consistently dry between changings, and more often than not going to the potty at changing time. Do not continue to ask, "Do you have to go potty?" if the child repeatedly denies the urge. Instead, after the child shows the signs of readiness, put the child on the pot at regular intervals during the day and praise him if he goes.

6. Day care drop-off

Erroneous Expectation: Parents expect their children to easily separate from them when the children are dropped off at school or day care.

The Reality: It is common for children ages eight to fourteen months to experience difficulty separating from their parents. Believe it or not, your children's crying or tantruming when you try to drop them off at day care or elsewhere may be a good sign that they have a strong relationship with you. Kids can also go through phases where they appear "clingy," but by age six they should separate comfortably from you.

What to Do: Prepare your child for the drop-off by making him feel more in control of the morning events or give him something to comfort him during the day, such as a family picture or a special blanket. Then become Master of the Quick Exit. Kiss the kids good-bye, tell them when you'll see them again, and get out of there! Call day care from work and ask how long it took your child to calm down.

7. Naps

Erroneous Expectation: Parents would like their children to take one- to two-hour afternoon naps until the age of ten or eleven!

The Reality: About 60 percent of children stop daily naps by age three; 80 percent stop by age five. As they get older, children sleep longer at night and less during the day. You will see more sleeping during the day as children go through growth spurts, get sick, or are working hard physically or cognitively.

What to Do: First, ensure a good nap environment with a calm-down routine and a dark and quiet room. Be consistent in your approach to nap time. Nap schedules are different for every child, so look for signs of fatigue. As your child gets older, instead of requiring that he fall sleep, ask your child to spend quiet time in his room. If he's tired, he will sleep. If not, he will relax and regroup.

8. Lying

Erroneous Expectation: Parents expect kids of all ages to tell the truth at all times.

The Reality: Just about everybody—kids and adults—lies at some time or another. Some research indicates that 20 percent of two-year-olds lie, as well as 50 percent of three-year-olds, 90 percent of four-year-olds, and 70 percent of sixteen-year-olds. The increasing percentages in the preschool crowd reflect a positive thing—increasing intellectual capacity! The most common reason for lying is to cover up mistakes or misbehavior.

What to Do: Don't treat lying as if it were a great crime. If you already know that a child did something wrong, don't "corner" him by asking questions when you already know the answers to see if he is going to tell the truth. Gently punish your child for lying if necessary. Most important, if a child regularly lies about a problem behavior (for example, not completing homework), fix the basic problem and the child will no longer feel compelled to lie about it.

9. Cleaning room and picking up

Erroneous Expectation: Parents expect their children to be able to immediately follow through with the instruction "clean your room" or "pick up your stuff."

The Reality: All children like making a mess, but few children of any age like picking up. Typically developing preschoolers cannot clean their rooms without supervision and praise. By grades two to three, children can straighten their room (with specific instructions given), as well as run errands or complete simple chores. By age six, children can complete chores up to twenty minutes in length and clean their room after a request.

What to Do: For children under the age of four, model appropriate chore completion by doing the task alongside your child at first. Provide a visual list of what you'd like done (like a 1-2-3 Magic chart or a series of simple pictures) and praise the child's accomplishments. For older children, consider the weekly cleanup routine, the garbage bag method, or the docking system.

10. Dinnertime: Sitting and eating

Erroneous Expectation: Parents expect their children of all ages to sit at the table, eat all of their dinner before dessert, and then ask to be excused.

The Reality: Surprisingly, sitting at the dinner table actually requires a lot of mental effort for kids! If they're hungry, most children can sit still and eat. If they're not hungry, our "three-minutes-per-year rule" kicks in. Two-year-olds who are full will sit for about six minutes, three-year-olds for about nine minutes, and five-year-olds for fifteen minutes. Some days children will eat tons and other days not much, depending on the amount of energy they've used.

What to Do: Use 1-2-3 Magic strategies for dinnertime. Keep portion sizes modest. Allow the little ones to say they're full and leave the table. If a child is full and declines dessert, that's OK! You can also consider removing dessert or offering only healthy options during the week. Finally, make mealtime fun! Play a guessing game, let your child help prepare food, and offer choices of utensils!

11. Homework

Erroneous Expectation: Parents expect children of all ages to start and complete homework independently.

The Reality: Six- to seven-year-olds can do about ten minutes of unsupervised homework. A useful expectation is to add roughly ten minutes of homework for each additional year. Research shows that children whose parents help with homework feel better about themselves and have better relationships with their teachers!

What to Do: Maintain an afternoon homework routine at a specific place and time. Allow your child to choose the order in which he completes homework. Consider using your 1-2-3 Magic charting for homework. Include one point for no complaining and one point for starting on their own without being reminded. Show interest in the kids' assignments.

12. Going to bed and staying there

Erroneous Expectation: Parents expect their kids to be able to get to sleep and stay asleep by themselves.

The Reality: Adequate sleep deeply affects children's development, emotions, attention, and school performance. Generally, children under five will not be able to both get themselves to bed and go to sleep on their own. Preschoolers often find going to bed simultaneously boring and frightening.

What to Do: Twenty to thirty minutes of your time will be required per night to help little ones through a consistent, reassuring, calm-down ritual. Determine a bedtime by consulting a "typical sleep requirements for various age groups" chart, then calculate backwards from the time the children have to get up in the morning. Use the 1-2-3 Magic Basic Bedtime Method and "cut them off at the pass" when necessary.

Know Your Child's Brain Limits!

Your child's brain is such an amazing thing, and it changes and matures so rapidly. It's easy to get your child and yourself into trouble by expecting too much.

By far the biggest problem expectation is the Little Adult Assumption. This assumption leads adults to use words and reasons in discipline situations with children who are too small to appreciate or respond well to them. At best, this premature logic simply irritates kids and confuses the situation. At worst, however, the Little Adult Assumption leads to Talk-Persuade-Argue-Yell-Hit! Syndrome.

Very unnecessary and very sad.

CHAPTER SUMMARY

This chapter is a bit like the Little Adult Assumption, isn't it? If you understand what kids are capable of at different ages, you're less likely to, on the one hand, think the kids are out to get you! On the other hand, understanding what's normal lets you know the kid's behavior is not your fault. Gently train and help your little ones to master new behaviors and self-control.

PART V

Strengthening Your Relationships with Your Children

Parenting Job 3

CHAPTER 19
Sympathetic Listening

CHAPTER 20
The Dangers of Over-Parenting

CHAPTER 21
Real Magic: One-on-One Fun

CHAPTER 22
Solving Problems Together

19
SYMPATHETIC LISTENING
Why It's Important to Hear What Your Children Have to Say

NOW WE TURN OUR attention to the final parenting job, strengthening your relationship with your children. Some people call this "bonding." If you bond well with your kids, the first two parenting jobs become easier. If you do the first two parenting jobs well, bonding will occur naturally. We'll discuss the two most powerful relationship-strengthening tactics—sympathetic listening and shared one-on-one fun—in the next two chapters.

Be a Good Listener

Your children will frequently surprise you with some of the things they say, and your first impulse often may be to react negatively. For example, your ten-year-old son, Tom, comes running in the door after school yelling, "My music teacher's an idiot!" What should you do? You may feel like saying, "That's no way to talk!" You could start counting—after all, the boy is screaming.

But think for a second. He is *not* screaming at you, and he *is* upset about something and you don't know what it is. Your priority? Find out what happened and give the child some support. Being angry is no crime, and his outburst couldn't be testing and manipulation, because you didn't do anything to frustrate him. Here is a time for some sympathetic listening. The conversation might go something like this:

Tom: "My music teacher's an idiot!"

Mom: "Tell me what happened."

Tom: "She made me sing in front of the whole stupid class, and only one other kid had to do it. All my friends were laughing at me!"

Mom: "What did she make you sing?"

Tom: "I don't know, some jerk hymn or something."

Mom: "That must have been awfully embarrassing."

Tom: "I'm going to flunk her class—on purpose!"

Mom: "Boy, I haven't seen you this mad for a while! So what happened when you had to sing?"

Tom: "She makes me stand in the front of the room, then she plays her idiot piano, and I don't even know the words! I could see Dave was giggling and trying not to laugh. I'd like to see him do it!"

Mom: "So you thought it wasn't right for her to make you do it when no one else had to."

Tom: "Yeah. Why are they picking on me all the time? What a totally ignorant school." *(Tom leaves to get a snack.)*

Sympathetic listening is a way of talking to someone with sympathy or empathy. (The distinction between the two isn't important here.) Listening is very respectful of another person's thoughts and feelings, because the listener doesn't just sit there but instead attempts to see the world through the other person's eyes.

When you are listening to your child, you are—like Tom's mother—forgetting your own opinions for a while, suspending judgment, and committing yourself to completely understanding how the child saw a particular situation. (You don't have to agree with him.) In our example, Mom is not assuming that her son is being disrespectful or that he caused the trouble. Nor is she formulating her own response.

Therefore, sympathetic listening should be done to accomplish two things: (1) to understand what another person is saying and thinking—from his or her point of view, and (2) to communicate back and check that understanding with the person doing the talking. The listener is an active participant in the conversation, not someone who just sits and nods from time to time (although that's not so bad either when you're totally beat!).

Sympathetic listening is not easy for parents. Once you get past the point of feeling artificial or passive, however, you can sometimes pleasantly surprise your children with your willingness to listen to their concerns and hear their side of the story. Listening is an excellent way to begin any lengthy, serious conversation, and being respectfully listened to is a great self-esteem builder for kids.

> **Quik Tip**
> Sympathetic listening is very respectful of your child's thoughts and feelings. But listening isn't easy—you have to learn to keep your own opinions to yourself for a while!

How Do You Do Sympathetic Listening?

There are several steps to sympathetic listening. First, you have to get yourself in the proper frame of mind: "I'm going to hear this kid out—even if it kills me—and find out exactly what he thinks." Then several different approaches can be used, and once you get used to them, the whole process should feel very natural. Your listening strategies include openers, nonjudgmental questions, reflecting feelings, and checks or summaries.

Openers

You can start with what are called "openers"—brief comments or questions designed to elicit further information from your child. These comments often require self-control and are especially difficult when you are caught off guard. Openers may also appear incredibly passive to you, but remember that parental listening must precede any problem-solving discussion. If discipline or other action is necessary, worry about that after you've gotten the facts.

Openers can be very simple, such as "Oh?" "Wow!" "Yeah" or "What?" An opener can be anything that communicates that you are ready and willing to listen sympathetically, including nonverbal behavior, such as sitting down next to the child or putting down the paper to look at him. In the example, Mom's opener was "Tell me what happened."

Nonjudgmental Questions

After openers, questions are often necessary to further your understanding of what a child is talking about. To be effective, these questions must not be loaded or judgmental. "Why did you do a stupid thing like that?" "What's your problem today?" or "Why are you bugging me now about this?" are not good questions. These comments will inspire arguments or silence.

Here are some better questions that continue the discussion and further understanding: "What do you think made you do that?" or "What was going through your mind at the time?" In our example, Mom asked Tom, "So what happened when you had to sing?" That was a good question.

Reflecting Feelings

A third sympathetic listening strategy is called "reflecting feelings." If you are going to tell someone that you think you understand him, try to let him know that you can imagine how he must have felt under the circumstances. Sometimes, when you reflect feelings, older kids will tell you that you sound a bit like a shrink. If that's the case, just say, "Sorry, but I'm just trying to make sure I understand what you're talking about."

In the example, Mom reflected Tom's feelings at two points: "That must have been awfully embarrassing" and "Boy, I haven't seen you this mad for a while!" Other examples of reflecting feelings might include: "You really sound bummed out about that," "That must have really been fun!" or "You were pretty upset with me."

The process of reflecting feelings accomplishes several things. First, it lets the child know that what he is feeling is OK. (It's what he may *do* about it that can be right or wrong.) Second, the reflecting response reinforces self-esteem and independence. And third, reflecting feelings also helps diffuse negative emotions so they are not acted out somewhere else. You can bet that if Tom's mother had first said, "That's no way to talk about your teachers!" his anger would have been redirected at her immediately.

Checks or Summaries

From time to time during a talk, it is helpful to check out whether or not you are really getting a good idea of what your child is saying. Giving short summaries now and then of what your child is telling you lets him know that you're really listening and trying to see the world for a moment through his eyes.

Examples of checks or summaries might be: "Sounds like you're saying that our rules for chores favor your sister," "You felt it was your worst day at school this year," or "You wish I weren't gone so much so we could do more together?" In the example above, Mom's summary was this: "So you thought it wasn't very fair for her to make you do it when no one else had to." That was a nice, sympathetic comment.

Good listening is a communication skill, but it is also an attitude—your attitude, not your child's. It's the attitude of sincerely trying to figure out what someone else is thinking even if you don't agree. This, of course, is a different kind of job if you're talking to a two-year-old or a ten-year-old. You'll also find that if you listen well, you learn a lot about what your children think about life. That's important as you monitor their psychological and emotional growth. Start listening now, because you'll certainly want to stay in touch with your kids when they're teens!

> **Quik Tip**
> Listening is a skill, but it's also an attitude—on your part. You'll learn a lot about what your kids think about life. Better start listening now, because you're definitely going to want to know what your kids are thinking when they're teenagers!

Sympathetic Listening and Counting

So listening helps you to understand your children and also helps to diffuse negative emotions. That's fine, but if you listened *all the time*, you wouldn't be any kind of a disciplinarian. Sympathetic listening by itself has very little to do with setting limits and enforcing rules. Imagine this scene:

> **Caution**
> 1. You are a **good listener** if, while your child is talking, you are sincerely trying to understand what he is saying.
> 2. You are a **bad listener** if, while your child is talking, you are preparing your rebuttal.

Son: "Mom—you idiot! My best T-shirt's still in the wash!"

Mother: "You're feeling pretty frustrated with me."

This parent's response is inappropriate. The child's disrespect is way out of proportion to the situation and should be confronted, probably by counting.

On the other hand, if you counted *all the time* whenever the kids were upset, you wouldn't be a very understanding parent. Your kids would correctly perceive you as only an instrument of discipline—or worse.

Imagine this summertime scenario:

"I'm bored."

"That's 1."

That's a pretty insensitive and unnecessary response. Your kids certainly won't want to talk to you very often! So how is a parent supposed to know when to listen and when to count? Sometimes this decision is easy, but often it's not. Our general guideline is this: discuss problems, count attacks.

Discuss Problems

When a child is upset about something but not being disrespectful to you, it's time to listen and discuss the problem. "Mom, my best T-shirt's still in the wash" might lead to a practical discussion of what to do about the clothing shortage.

Or try this. In the car on the way to soccer practice, your

eleven-year-old son says, "Our family is so boring." You might want to say, "You're not so hot yourself." Wrong. You should listen and be sympathetic. "I've never heard you say that before. What's on your mind?" is better.

Some children's comments may give you pause, but they're not really attacks. If a parent uses a little active listening, the emotion may be diffused:

"Why are you making me do this stupid homework now?"
"Homework's a real bummer, isn't it?" (Reflecting feeling)
"Oh, brother." *(Child starts his homework with a sigh.)*
Happy ending for parent; semi-happy ending for kid.

Count Attacks

"Mom—you idiot—my best T-shirt's still in the wash!" is an attack from the start, and many parents would give an immediate 3 for the "idiot" remark.

Sometimes listening doesn't work as well as you'd like. Keep the 1-2-3 strategy ready in your back pocket. The homework conversation might have gone like this:

"Why are you making me do this stupid homework now?"
"Homework's a real bummer, isn't it?" (Reflecting)
"Yeah, I hate it!"
"Boy, you really don't like it, do you?" (Reflecting)
"I could be rollerblading with Jason."
"You'd really prefer to be outside playing." (Summary)
"Don't just say back everything I say!"
"That's 1."

Real-Life Story 4

SYMPATHETIC LISTENING

A big piece of Parenting Job 3, strengthening your relationships with your children, is listening to what your kids have to say. You want to be a good listener when your children are happy and excited, but it's also important to be there for them when they're frustrated, sad, or upset.

Unfortunately, sympathetic listening is easier to describe than it is to do. Sometimes we don't have the time to listen. At other times, we simply don't remember to take the time when we really could.

In our Real-Life Story 4, *The Case of the Fickle Friends*, you will see me mishandle a situation in which my son was temporarily upset with some of his neighborhood buddies. In the portion of the story called the **Wrong Way**, you'll see me being a lousy listener. In **Thinking It Through**, we'll take a look at what I messed up. Then we'll give you a chance to evaluate your own listening skills with your kids.

Finally, the **Right Way** section of our narrative will give me a chance to undo my mistake—an opportunity that doesn't always happen in real life!

THE CASE OF THE FICKLE FRIENDS

When my wife and I got our first house, we were thrilled to death. Not only did we have our own yard, but our kids would also have neighborhood friends to play with. What wasn't so thrilling, however, was our introduction to the new and unfamiliar world of playtime politics.

WRONG WAY

THINKING IT THROUGH

As I watched my son walk away, I realized that I had just blown it. Although I was caught off guard, what I said and did simply made matters worse.

WELL DON'T BOTHER ME ABOUT IT. FIND SOMETHING ELSE TO DO.

He was looking for a little reassurance and support, but I was too busy and aggravated to provide it for him.

To make matters worse, I misused the strategy of counting. Not very sympathetic, was I!

STOP WHINING. THAT'S 1.

GEE, THANKS, DAD.

Listening to your youngsters is important. It's important for children's self-esteem and it's important for you to know what your kids are thinking. Let's revisit **The Case of the Fickle Friends** and give me a second chance to do it right.

RIGHT WAY

RIGHT WAY

Being angry is no crime.

A sympathetic question was a better way to start.

Here I turned around and took time to listen. I gave my son emotional support, but at the same time I let him solve his own problem.

Better ending. David's less upset, I'm less upset —most important—we're not mad at each other.

GOOD JOB, DAD!

Your Child's Instinctive Emotional Repertoire

Your child experiencing negative emotions is not a crime. As a matter of fact, psychologists these days are taking a new look at human emotion. They see emotion, positive and negative, as a critical part of the problem-solving process along with—and not instead of—information processing. The current thought is that, in addition to providing spice to life, emotions are providing a very necessary motivational component to problem solving.

In a part of the brain called the amygdala, your child's brain is prewired from birth to be able to produce or feel a wide variety of emotions. The amygdala in your child's brain is also involved with memory and motivation. When you listen with interest and sympathy to your kids, you help them understand and manage feelings and behavior. Keep in mind that warm and demanding parenting is best for your child's neurological development, so sometimes you need to lend an ear and at other times you need to set limits. Not an easy job!

CHAPTER SUMMARY

Sympathetic listening is a wonderful parental activity for several reasons. First, it's a really nice thing to do for your kids. Second, it makes you a safe haven for your children—someone they'll want to turn to when they're upset. And finally, good listening skills on your part mean that you will stay in touch with your kids' thoughts and feelings. Adolescence is not far off!

20

THE DANGERS OF OVER-PARENTING

Knowing When to Let Your Kids Think for Themselves

ANOTHER GOOD WAY TO strengthen a relationship is to avoid what we call over-parenting. Over-parenting consists of unnecessary corrective, cautionary, or disciplinary comments, and can result in a parent forcing unnecessary comments down a kid's throat, making the child feel aggravated and put down. While sympathetic listening encourages independence, over-parenting discourages it. Parent squawks, kid "listens."

A while back, I was in a grocery store standing in front of the dairy case. As I was trying to decide which kind of milk to buy, I noticed a mother with her daughter, about nine years old, who was pushing a cart and coming around the corner toward me. As they came closer, the mother said loudly and anxiously, "Now watch out for that man over there!"

I'm an average-sized guy; there was no way this girl was not going to see me. Even if she had been traveling at 40 miles per hour, she would still have had plenty of room to stop before breaking my legs. Mom's comment was an example of over-parenting.

Adults who over-parent usually do it repeatedly, and over-parenting has predictable, negative effects on children. The first negative reaction is what we call the "Anxious Parent, Angry Child" syndrome. Continually expressing unnecessary worries about kids *to* the kids irritates the children because it insults them. The parent's basic message is this: "I have to worry about you so much because you're incompetent. There's not much you can do on your own without my supervision and direction." No child likes to be put down, and over-parenting is definitely a put-down. Over-parenting comments can be unnecessary for several reasons:

1. The child already has the skill necessary to manage the situation. Example: the little girl in my grocery-store story.
2. Even if the child doesn't have all the necessary skills to manage the situation, it would be preferable for him or her to learn by direct experience. When we moved into our first house, the kids were about two and four. I'd watch them playing outside with other children, and every five minutes or so I'd see some kind of dispute that I thought needed my intervention. Then one day my wife asked me how I thought the kids survived all day while I was at work. No eyes poked out, no broken arms, no deaths. That shut me up. I'd been over-parenting the whole neighborhood.
3. The issue is not important enough to warrant parent intervention. For example, Mike and Jimmy are out in the front yard playing catch with a baseball. Jimmy's dad is washing the car in the driveway while the neighbor, Mr. Smith, is cutting his grass next door. Mike misses Jimmy's throw and the ball rolls over toward Mr. Smith, who smiles and tosses it back. Dad tells the two boys they will have to go somewhere else or stop playing catch. Should Dad have kept quiet? Yes, he should have. Let the two lads work it out with Mr. Smith, if necessary. The boys were having innocent, constructive fun,

and Mr. Smith probably enjoyed trying out his old pitching arm again!

You certainly want your kids to comply with your house rules, but as the years go by, you want something else from them more and more: *independence*. Your children have to leave you someday, and you must help them get ready for that huge event. Being a good listener and avoiding over-parenting are great ways to help your kids prepare for adulthood.

Independence and Self-Esteem

You are looking for two big things from your children as they grow up. One is for them to cooperate—comply with the rules, limit obnoxious behavior, and do what they're supposed to do.

But another equally important trait you want from them—believe it or not—is independence. From whom? From you! Your kids are going to leave home someday, and when they do, you want them to be able to think for themselves, make their own decisions, and manage their own lives.

Growing autonomy contributes in a big way to children's self-esteem. And children seek out—and push for—independence very assertively, as any parent of a two-year-old knows! By directly limiting, undermining, or even attacking a child's powerful drive for autonomy, unwitting moms and dads will put a huge dent in their child's emerging self-esteem.

Overparenting

Kids' brains are wired from birth to motivate behavior that involves movement, experimentation, and exploration. Unfortunately, such behavior in kids often stimulates anxious responses in the brains of their parents, who can then become overly restrictive and oppressive.

Safety concerns are very real issues with small children, and knowing how to childproof a house and when to count risky behavior are critical skills for moms and dads. Just as important, though, is knowing when and how to let your child's brain investigate and interact with the big, bad world. Enjoy the show!

CHAPTER SUMMARY

Too often over-parenting is simply an anxious, knee-jerk response from a parent. Kids can get really tired of feeling insulted. Before opening your mouth, do some brutally honest reflection on whether or not your opinion is really needed.

21
REAL MAGIC: ONE-ON-ONE FUN

The Best Thing You Can Do for Your Kids

SHOW ME ANY TWO people who have fun together frequently, and I'll show you a good relationship. Shared fun provides necessary nutrition for a personal relationship. Whether they are young or old, people who have regular fun together tend to like each other. For many families these days, however, this much-needed one-on-one enjoyment gets put on the back burner because of the unfortunate focus on two things: work and whole-family activities.

Work, Work, Work

Do you remember how you got married? Most of us started out by dating another person. By and large, that meant having fun. Dating was going to the movies, eating at restaurants, endless getting-to-know-you talks, travel, shopping, parties with friends, and a whole host of other activities.

Then we went on to make what was perhaps one of the most illogical decisions of our entire existence. We reasoned as follows: Think of all the fun we're having now, and we're not even married. We're only together *half* of the time. Once we're together *all* the time, our good times will double!

That's what we believed. What was illogical about that thought had to do with the fact that getting married is fundamentally a decision to *work together*. Now we'll plan the wedding, now we'll get jobs, now we'll have a baby, now we'll buy a condo, now we'll decorate the condo. The former fun got subordinated to work. Gradually you realized your relationship was getting more strained, and you looked at your spouse one day and thought: "You're not as much fun as you used to be."

In the long run, of course, marriage is a mixture of work and play. The successful couples are the ones who can find the happy balance. But since work fills our time so naturally and aggressively, finding that balance really boils down to maintaining sufficient time for shared fun. If you asked me what's more important in a long-term relationship, communication or shared fun, I would answer "Fun."

The same is true in your relationship with each of your children. To like your kids, you must enjoy them regularly. And for them to respond positively to your discipline, they should enjoy and like you. Yes, there is work to be done, but it is absolutely critical that you find time to play.

> **Quik Tip**
>
> To like your kids you must enjoy them regularly. And for them to respond well to your discipline, they must enjoy and like you too. That means only one thing: you'd better find regular time to play with your children!

Unfortunately, in the hustle and bustle of everyday existence, many of the daily encounters between parent and child go something like this:

"Time to get up."

"Here's your breakfast. No TV until you're done."

"Got your book bag?"

"You don't have time to play with the dog."

"Come on now, we're in a hurry!"

"Don't forget your coat."
"Love you, good-bye."
The parent sees the child as a bundle of unpleasant tasks, and the child sees the parent as a bundle of unpleasant directions. No relationship will remain healthy when this kind of interaction is the only feeding it gets.

The Problem with the Focus on Whole-Family Activities

Brace yourself for some bad news: family fun today is way overrated. We consistently hear, for example, that eating dinner as a family every night is a surefire way of preventing crime, drug abuse, academic underachievement, teenage pregnancy, and a bunch of other social challenges.

But sometimes going out with the whole crew is not all it's cracked up to be for three reasons. The first is sibling rivalry. Mom and Dad are at the beach, for instance. Their six-year-old son says something rude to his eight-year-old sister, who throws her hot dog at her brother, who laughs as it misses and gets full of sand. Now both kids are screaming at each other, and everyone on the beach is staring. That isn't fun.

The second reason fun with the entire family doesn't always work is because the more people you put together in the same place, the greater the chance for differences of opinion and conflict. At 9:30 a.m. on the second day of their family vacation, for example, Mark wants to go to Creature Castle, Cynthia wants to go to the pool, Mom wants to have a leisurely cup of coffee, and Dad wants to jog three miles.

The final reason family fun is overrated is because the best parent-child bonding occurs in one-on-one parent-child interactions. Children cherish alone time with a mother or father, without the presence of their greatest rivals—their siblings. They open up, they feel free, and they kind of blossom. It would be a shame to rarely—or never—experience that kind of bonding with each of your children individually.

Play with Your Child

It's very important, therefore, to take your kids, one at a time, and regularly do something you both like. It's more peaceful because there's no fighting between siblings, and coordinating different agendas is no problem because there are only two agendas to coordinate.

The possibilities for shared one-on-one fun are endless. Many parents I've worked with over the years like to take one child out to dinner on a school night while everyone else stays home. Going to a movie, shopping, bike riding, or just going out for a drive in the car are also positive activities to do together. One of the nice things about getting out of the house is that no one can interrupt you. Your kids will also like it if you turn off your cell phone while you're out with them.

One-on-one fun, though, does not have to entail going out, nor does it have to involve spending money. Shared fun can come in little bits and pieces during the day. Moments of fun can be shared and enjoyed when you are talking, listening, expressing affection, or telling jokes. Most children love being able to stay up twenty minutes later on a school night every now and then to do something special with Mom or Dad. That something might be reading, just talking or—heaven forbid!—teaching a naive and inexperienced parent how to play a video game.

The moral of this chapter? By all means, do things together with the entire family, but make sure those times are as enjoyable as possible. If whole-family activities are usually miserable experiences, fix them! But whatever you do about whole-family fun, make sure your days and weeks include regular one-on-one fun with each of your children.

Fun Is Not a Waste of Time!

Moments of shared fun and affection between you and your child have a big effect on your child's maturing brain. Scientists believe that such positive times create a hormone called oxytocin in the brains of both adults and children. This type of bonding on a regular basis helps inoculate your child's nervous system from stress and can provide lifelong positive outcomes.

When it comes to constructive impacts on growing brains, actions and time speak louder than words. Saying "I love you" is fine, but it only takes a moment. A deeper positive impression will be made by engaging in shared one-on-one fun for extended periods of time with each of your little ones. Profound parent-child bonding will also occur every time you manage Stop and Start behavior well. That's real brainpower for the future!

CHAPTER SUMMARY
One-on-One Time
The best parent-child bonding occurs during one-on-one fun times. Why? For the kids, they have you all to themselves! And for you, there's absolutely no chance for sibling rivalry. Now there's a formula for success!

22
SOLVING PROBLEMS TOGETHER
Why It's Better to Work as a Team

WHEN YOUR CHILDREN ARE small, you should be the boss. Your parenting should be a kind of benevolent dictatorship where you make most of the decisions, you are the judge and jury, and you are gentle and kind. Your children will not decide each day what they have for dinner, when they go to bed, or whether or not they show up for preschool in the morning.

As your little ones get older, however, the setup should gradually change. When your children are seventeen, the household should be almost, but not quite, a democracy. Almost a democracy means that your adolescents have a lot more to say about the rules and policies that affect them. This notion also means that as the years have gone by, you have been giving your kids more and more independence. Ideally, teens should be making their own decisions about homework, bedtime, choice of friends, clothes and—to a large extent—diet. *Encouraging children's growing independence* is one of a parent's most important challenges.

How do you go about supporting your kids' independence? First, you avoid over-parenting, and second, you involve your kids in problem-solving efforts through family meetings and one-on-one parent-child meetings.

These get-togethers are a good idea for several reasons. As the kids get older it makes more sense that they have a bigger voice regarding the issues that affect them. In addition, kids will cooperate better with a decision or policy when they have had a say in the development of that idea. And finally, children need the experience of family negotiation to prepare for managing their own marriages and families. Unfortunately, far too many married adults learn the hard way—when it is too late—that their personal negotiation skills could use some work.

A good time to start family or one-on-one meetings is when the kids are around first grade. Don't try meetings when the children are three or four years old, as they'll be too young to understand the process. The family meeting can take place as often as you wish; once every week or two is ideal. One-on-one conferences should be done less frequently, or as needed. You can call special meetings whenever a unique problem comes up, and your kids can also request a meeting themselves.

How to Run a Family Meeting

The format of the family meeting is simple. One parent is usually the chairperson and has responsibility for keeping order and keeping people on task. Older children can try running the meeting themselves from time to time if you think they can handle the job. The chairperson sees to it that the agenda is followed, that each person gets a chance to speak, and that others listen without interrupting.

What is the agenda? Each person in the family brings to the meeting a problem that he or she wants resolved. Then, with each issue, the chairperson guides the group through the following steps:

1. The first speaker describes the problem she wants resolved.
2. One by one, every other person gives his or her thoughts and feelings about that issue. Others try hard to listen.
3. The floor is opened to proposals for solutions; anyone can speak, but only one at a time.
4. A solution to be tried is agreed upon. This final idea may combine aspects of suggestions from different people. If there are disagreements, Mom and Dad have the final say.
5. The solution is entered in the computer, and a hard copy is posted on the refrigerator.
6. Next person, next problem; steps 2–5 are repeated.

Most solutions are considered experimental, especially if the plan is complex and differences of opinion are large. If the proposed resolution doesn't work, that idea will be reviewed at the next family meeting. Although proposals should be concrete, specific, and practical, don't be afraid to make them flexible and imaginative! (See *The Case of the Disappearing Soda* section in this chapter.)

Sitting through these family meetings is not always easy. If you're hoping these will be warm, fuzzy experiences, they're not. In fact, family meetings can be downright obnoxious, so it's a good idea to keep them under an hour long. Before our family meetings, our kids would grumble and tell us that all their friends thought my wife and I were weird. But once they were at the meeting, neither of them would hesitate to put in their two cents!

The Case of the Disappearing Soda

When she was nine, my daughter brought this weighty issue to our biweekly family meeting. She explained we usually bought an eight-pack of soda pop, and there were four people in the family. The problem was that she wasn't getting her two bottles. There was never any left! We all listened to our daughter's description of the problem, then Brother, Mom, and Dad all threw in their opinions.

After some jockeying around, we found a solution. When the

eight-pack of pop entered the house, all eight bottles would be initialed with a marker: two for Mom, two for Dad, two for Sister, and two for Brother. If you drank your two bottles, you were done until the next eight-pack arrived. If you still wanted more pop, you first had to check the eight-pack to see if there were any full bottles left. If there was a full one, you could purchase it for a certain amount from the person who "owned" it. If the person declined to sell, no testing and manipulation was allowed. This agreement was posted on the refrigerator, and it worked like a charm.

> **Quik Tip**
> Many parents agree that the family meeting is one of the most *aggravating* and one of the most *effective* things you can do with your children. Don't ever expect anyone to want to come!

How to Do a One-on-One Meeting

What if you are concerned about just one of your children and not the whole family? When are you supposed to talk? Imagine you have become concerned about the way that your eight-year-old son has been treating his friends when they come over to play. Two things bother you: (1) he makes fun of the other boys, and (2) he will only play what he wants to play and will not listen to any suggestions.

What do you do? You make an appointment with your son and calmly and briefly tell him what you are worried about. For example, "I'm concerned about how you've been playing with Mark and Kyle. Let's get together some time and talk about it." Then you get together, just the two of you, and follow the family meeting format described earlier in this chapter.

1. **Describe the problem.** Be brief—no nagging or lecturing. "I'm concerned about you making fun of your friends and not letting them do what they want to do when they're at our house."

2. **Ask your son for his opinion of the situation.** "What do you think about this?" Do your best sympathetic listening.
3. **Generate some solutions.** "What can we do about this, and how can I help out?" Wait for your child to come up with ideas first. If he can't or he refuses, then come up with your own.
4. **Agree** on something to try and be very specific.

You don't need to enter the solution in the computer unless your son wants to. Try out the ideas, praise cooperation, and fine-tune the agreement in future meetings. Helpful hints: before the meeting make sure you're in a good mood; during the meeting make sure your listening shoes are on; and after the summit try a little shared one-on-one fun. Good luck!

Solving Problems Together

The part of your brain and of your child's brain that is involved in solving problems is the prefrontal cortex. This part of your child's brain integrates conceptual, emotional, and social input when it is trying to decide what to do. Many mental health professionals believe that being able to solve problems and minimize anxiety is critical to a healthy, growing brain.

Whenever you count difficult behavior like whining or tantrums, or whenever you set up constructive routines for positive behavior like homework or going to bed, you are helping your child's brain learn how to solve problems. And as your children get older, you'll find it more and more profitable to sit down either as a family or in a one-on-one setting to talk over and resolve living-together issues. Your child's prefrontal cortex is growing up capable and healthy!

CHAPTER SUMMARY

Family meetings and one-on-one meetings are not always fun. But they help prepare your kids for one of life's ultimate challenges... living with someone else!

PART VI

Enjoying Your New Family Life

CHAPTER 23
Staying Consistent

CHAPTER 24
Your Happy, Healthy Family

23
STAYING CONSISTENT

You Will Make Some Mistakes— and That's Okay!

BY THIS POINT YOU should be well into your three parenting jobs. You are controlling obnoxious behavior with counting, you are using the seven Start behavior tactics to establish positive routines, and you are consistently working on reinforcing your relationships with each of your children. 1-2-3 Magic is known for producing results. It works—and it often works in a very short time. No magic. Just the logical, consistent application of certain basic principles of parenting technology to the *n*th degree. But like any good thing in life, the 1-2-3 program takes some work and some thought to keep it going well.

Falling Off the Wagon

Parents are human beings who have good days and bad days. Many people have used the 1-2-3 program religiously for years and years. For other caregivers it is a struggle to stay consistent and remember what they're supposed to be doing.

The problem we're talking about here is called "slipping," or falling off the wagon. It means you start out well with 1-2-3 Magic, get the kids shaped up, but then slip back into your old unproductive ways of operating. The 1-2-3 Magic switch goes to the off position. The former status quo has a nasty way of sneaking back up on us. Falling off the wagon can occur suddenly on an especially bad day, or slipping can happen more gradually over months or even years.

In the course of a day there's always so much going on. You have to go to work, drive the kids all over the place, feed everybody, answer phone calls, help with homework, call your mother, and try to find a little time to read the paper. When you're doing nine things at once, who can remember the No Talking and No Emotion Rules? *You* can! It's not always easy, but it beats arguing and screaming, which only add to your troubles and make you feel angry and guilty later. Remember: *1-2-3 Magic* was written for busy parents like yourself who are inevitably going to get upset from time to time.

Quik Tip
When you're doing nine things at once, who can remember the No Talking and No Emotion Rules? You can!

Over the long term, slipping can occur for a number of reasons. The most frequent culprits are visitors, illness, travel, new babies, and plain forgetfulness. Gradually you find yourself talking too much, forgetting your Start behavior routines, and not enjoying your kids anymore. Then one night, you wake up at 3:00 a.m. and wonder, "What happened to the 1-2-3 method?"

Emotional Obstacles

Slipping can also occur in certain situations where your thoughts and emotions conspire to throw you off track. In these situations, it's not so much that you forget what you should do. Instead, emotional forces inside, caused by a little bit of screwy thinking, push you toward a bad discipline response.

How do you manage these unwanted tests of your will? Clear thinking—along with a little effort and courage—is often needed. Let's look at a few examples.

Anxiety: What will people think?

Wrong way: You have two other couples over for dinner, and you're sitting at the table with them and your son and daughter, ages six and eight. The kids start poking one another. Daughter pushes Son and says, "Leave me alone!" One of your guests laughs and says nervously, "Well, kids are always kids, aren't they?" *You think,* "I don't want to embarrass myself and everyone else by disciplining my kids at the dinner table." *You laugh along* with your friend.

Right way: *You think,* "Our friends may wonder what I'm doing, but I'd better nip this fight in the bud." *You say,* "Guys, you're both on a 1." Then you briefly explain counting to your guests.

Anger: Bringing your work home

Wrong way: You've had a terrible day at work, having made two major mistakes and aggravating your boss big time. When you walk in the door, the kids are watching TV and the family room floor is covered with books, papers, pens, toys, and just general junk. *You think,* "Why can't these kids ever put anything away?" *You yell,* "What's the matter with you guys! THIS ISN'T A PIGPEN. IT'S SUPPOSED TO BE A HOME!"

Right way: *You think,* "I'm a walking time bomb waiting to go off. Kids are kids, and we'll worry about picking up at eight o'clock like we usually do." *You say,* "Hi, guys. I've had a terrible day and need a little space for a few minutes."

Guilt: The poor kid!

Wrong way: It's 2:30 p.m. on a long, boring summer day. Your nine-year-old son asks you to buy him the new, all-the-rage video game. It's not that expensive. *You reply,* "Not today." He whimpers, "I never get to do anything. This summer really sucks!" *You think,* "I never liked the way my parents treated me. Poor kid. Why am I being so selfish?" *You say,* "All right, but that's all we're getting. I have work to do!"

Right way: *You think,* "His whimpering is Testing Tactic 4, martyrdom. He needs to develop more constructive ways of entertaining himself." *You say* nothing.

Sadness: Poor me

Wrong way: Two weeks ago your best friend of fourteen years moved from down the block to a city nine hundred miles away. It's 9:15 p.m., which is usually story time for your eight-year-old daughter and part of her basic bedtime routine. But over the last couple of weeks you've skipped story time on three occasions and had her go to sleep by herself. You hear, "Mom, are you coming up?" *You think,* "What's the use? I'm tired. She can get herself to sleep." *You say,* "Not tonight, honey."

Right way: *You think,* "I've been sloppy lately with her bedtime because of things going on in my own life. Maintaining the routine and our time together is important. I'll also feel better reading to her than I will sitting down here moping." *You say,* "I'll be up in a second."

Recovering from a Slip-Up

What do you do when you find yourself—over the short or long term—falling back into your old ways? First of all, *accept slipping as normal*. Nobody's perfect, including you, and you shouldn't expect yourself to be. Life—especially with kids—is also more complex, messy, and challenging than any of us ever anticipated.

Second, it's *back to basics*. Most often, when parents come to me and say "The 1-2-3 is not working anymore," what is happening is a violation of the No Talking and No Emotion Rules. The next most common setback is forgetting Parenting Job 3, relationship strengthening. So we sit down and review 1-2-3 Magic carefully, and then send Mom and Dad on their way. This brief refresher course usually takes care of the problem.

The fact that you used 1-2-3 Magic once and got tripped up a little does not hurt the program's effectiveness the second time around. Turn that 1-2-3 switch back to On.

When you have caught yourself backsliding, say something like this to your kids: "Guys, I'm not doing my job right. You got me frustrated, and I'm talking and yelling too much. We're going back to counting." When you've regressed over a longer period, consider redoing the Kickoff Conversation.

Over the course of your kids' growing-up time at your house, you may go through a number of slip-ups and recoveries—daily, monthly, or even annually. Each time you catch yourself getting careless, just pick yourself up, take a deep breath, and go back to what you know works best.

Steady as She Goes!

Your child's behavioral and corresponding neurological development depends a lot on your ability to put a healthy warm-and-demanding philosophy into your parenting efforts. Some situations, for example, call for praise and affection, while other situations call for limit setting by means of counting or simply saying no.

Life itself, however, with its inevitable ups and downs, doesn't always cooperate with your ideal parenting agenda, and you will from time to time slip up and either (1) forget to do something you should do (e.g., praise or fun) or (2) accidentally do something you should not do (e.g., yell or blame). The good thing about *1-2-3 Magic* is that the program makes it easy to recover from your mistakes so you can resume caring for and guiding your child's powerful, sensitive brain.

CHAPTER SUMMARY

One of the nice things about 1-2-3 Magic is that it's so easy to get back to. The most critical thing is to cut out all that extra talking! Remember: to slip up is human; to recover, divine.

24
YOUR HAPPY, HEALTHY FAMILY

How 1-2-3 Magic Will Change Your Life

WHAT CAN YOU EXPECT from 1-2-3 Magic? You can expect a more peaceful household, a lot less arguing, and fewer angry moments. You can expect to have more fun, and affection will come more easily. Your children's self-esteem will improve and so will yours. You will feel more in control and you will know you are handling parenting challenges correctly.

What it all boils down to is this: How do you want to spend your time with your kids? One option is that you can spend your time like this:

BEFORE 1-2-3 MAGIC

In this scenario, the kids are driving you crazy most of the time. You are caught up in frequent but futile attempts at "discipline." There is little time to enjoy your children, educate them, or even like them.

On the other hand, you can put some real thought and effort into establishing the 1-2-3 Magic program in your family and spend your time like this:

In this situation the proper parenting and family perspective has been established. Sanity is restored by the 1-2-3 system, making discipline crisp, gentle, and efficient. There's less arguing and yelling, and in this more peaceful atmosphere there are more good times. Everyone's self-esteem benefits.

"1-2-3 Magic Saved My Marriage"

I'll never forget the following story that one mother told me many years ago. 1-2-3 Magic brings families closer together—kids get along better with their siblings, and parents can even get along better with each other.

Michelle and her husband, Jack, had very different parenting styles. He was a spanker and she was a talker. They disagreed on what behaviors to discipline and on how to discipline them. Michelle tended to be too soft; Jack tended to be too hard. Each tried to overcompensate to make up for the other. It was a mess.

Michelle told me that she and Jack often argued about other things instead of the real issue. If her husband was too hard on their eight-year-old son, Kyle, while he was doing his homework, for instance, Michelle would nag about the laundry. If her husband thought she was too soft about homework, he would get snippy over the dishes. The two never said what the real problem was, and on the rare occasions that they did, it turned into a huge fight.

One time at the grocery store, Michelle temporarily got separated from Kyle and Dad. When she found them again, Kyle's eyes were red and he was rubbing his bottom.

"What happened?" Michelle asked as she glared at her husband.

"Daddy spanked me!" Kyle piped up.

"Why did Daddy spank you?" Mom asked.

Jack jumped in, "He wandered away from me and I couldn't find him."

Michelle gave her husband her best "I-am-so-mad-at-you" look. They then walked around the store fighting with each other in front of their son. Their conversation sounded like this:

"If you would just let me discipline him, he wouldn't run away like that."

"If you were watching him better, he wouldn't have run away."

"If you wouldn't be so soft on him, then he would listen the first time."

"If you wouldn't beat him, then he wouldn't want to run away."

This couple was going nowhere. Then one day, their pediatrician recommended a program with a strange name: 1-2-3 Magic. Michelle read the book and persuaded Jack to watch the DVD. After that, things changed fairly quickly.

As Michelle put it, "When we started 1-2-3 Magic, our parenting issues came together. And something else amazing happened. There was a lot less bickering about laundry and dishes. We didn't fight as much as we had before. Since using 1-2-3, our marriage is stronger and our parenting is simple and understood."

Differences in child-rearing tactics between

> **Good Luck!**
> Don't spend any more days caught up in useless irritation. Take charge of your home today—and start having some fun with your kids!

Mom and Dad can put terrible strains on marriages. As Michelle put it, "Now the expectations are the same for both of us, and the difference in our marriage (as well as in parenting our son) has been amazing."

Tap into Your Brain's Hardwiring!

One of the nice things about being a parent is that your brain is wired to see small children as cute—very, very cute. Often, people use the word *adorable* to describe little kids. Where exactly does this quality of cuteness exist? If you really think about it, it doesn't exist in the child; it exists in your brain. A large, predatory cat, for example, would see a child not as cute but as food.

The moments in which you see your children as cute or adorable are fun and they are priceless times. You want to maximize them. You want to enjoy watching the show that is the manifestation of your child's growing, changing brainpower. In addition to the lovability you see, however, kids' brains naturally produce whining, pouting, tantrums, screaming, and other obnoxious behavior. Use *1-2-3 Magic* in your new life to minimize these occasions and maximize the adorable ones!

APPENDIX
Further Readings and Resources

Emotional Intelligence

Borba, Michele. *Building Moral Intelligence: The Seven Essential Virtues That Teach Kids to Do the Right Thing.* San Francisco: Jossey-Bass, 2002.

Goleman, Daniel. *Emotional Intelligence: Why It Can Matter More Than IQ.* New York: Bantam Books, 2005.

Active Listening and Problem Solving

Faber, Adele, and Elaine Mazlish. *How to Talk So Kids Will Listen and Listen So Kids Will Talk.* New York: Scribner, 2012.

Ginott, Haim. *Between Parent and Child.* Revised and updated by Alice Ginott and H. Wallace Goddard. New York: Crown Publishing, 2003.

Childhood Emotional Problems

Chansky, Tamar E. *Freeing Your Child from Anxiety: Powerful, Practical Solutions to Overcome Your Child's Fears, Worries, and Phobias.* New York: Crown Publishing, 2014.

Coloroso, Barbara. *The Bully, the Bullied, and the Bystander: From Preschool to High School—How Parents and Teachers Can Help Break the Cycle.* New York: William Morrow Paperbacks, 2009.

Turecki, Stanley, and Sarah Warnick. *The Emotional Problems of Normal Children: How Parents Can Understand and Help.* New York: Bantam Books, 1994.

Separation and Divorce

Philyaw, Deesha, and Michael D. Thomas. *Co-Parenting 101: Helping Your Kids Thrive in Two Households after Divorce.* Oakland, CA: New Harbinger, 2013.

Ricci, Isolina. *The CoParenting Toolkit: The Essential Supplement for Mom's House, Dad's House.* La Vergne, TN: Lightning Source, 2015.

Tech and Media

Awareness Technologies. WebWatcherKids website, www.webwatcherkids.com (*Information on monitoring software*)

Common Sense Media website, www.commonsensemedia.org (*One-stop shop for reviews on TV, movies, music, games, books, and websites—excellent resource*)

McAfee. InternetSafety website, www.internetsafety.com (*Safe Eyes Internet filter*)

National Center for Missing and Exploited Children. NetSmartz website, www.netsmartz.org (*Very popular safety site used by educators, law enforcement, and parents*)

WiredSafety website, www.wiredsafety.org (*Internet safety site*)

Parenting Styles

Cohen, Lawrence J. *The Opposite of Worry: The Playful Parenting Approach to Childhood Anxieties and Fears.* New York: Ballantine Books, 2013.

Miles, Karen. *The Power of Loving Discipline.* New York: Penguin, 2006.

Semmelroth, Carl. *The Anger Habit in Parenting: A New Approach to Understanding and Resolving Family Conflict.* Naperville, IL: Sourcebooks, 2005.

Stiffelman, Susan. *Parenting with Presence: Practices for Raising Conscious, Confident, Caring Kids.* Novato, CA: New World Library, 2015.

Child Temperament

Borsky, Bari. *Authentic Parenting: A Four Temperaments Guide to Understanding Your Child—And Yourself!* Herndon, VA: SteinerBooks, 2013.

Dodson, James C. *The New Strong-Willed Child.* Carol Stream, IL: Tyndale Momentum, 2014.

Other Discipline Alternatives

Farber, Adele, and Elaine Mazlish. *Siblings without Rivalry: How to Help Your Children Live Together So You Can Live Too.* New York: W. W. Norton & Company, 2012.

Leman, Kevin. *Have a New Kid by Friday! How to Change Your Child's Attitude, Behavior & Character in 5 Days.* Grand Rapids, MI: Revell, 2012.

MacKenzie, Robert J. *Setting Limits with Your Strong-Willed Child: Eliminating Conflict by Establishing Clear, Firm, and Respectful Boundaries.* New York: Three Rivers Press, 2013.

Markham, Laura. *Peaceful Parent, Happy Kids: How to Stop Yelling and Start Connecting.* New York: Perigee, 2012.

Research on 1-2-3 Magic

Allen, Sharon M., Roy H. Thompson, and Jane Drapeaux. "Successful Methods for Increasing and Improving Parent and Child Interactions." Paper presented at the 24th Annual Training Conference of the National Head Start Association, Boston, May 25–31, 1997.

Bradley, Susan, Darryle-Anne Jadaa, Joel Brody, Sarah Landry, Susan E. Tallett, William Watson, Barbara Shea, et al. "Brief Psychoeducational Parenting Program: An Evaluation and 1-Year Follow-Up." *Journal of the American Academy of Child and Adolescent Psychiatry* 42, no. 10 (October 2003): 1171–78. doi:10.1097/01.chi.0000081823.25107.75.

Elgar, Frank J., and Patrick J. McGrath. "Self-Administered Psychosocial Treatments for Children and Families." *Journal of Clinical Psychology* 59, no. 3 (2003): 321–39. doi:10.1002/jclp.10132.

Norcross, John C., Linda F. Campbell, John M. Gohol, John W. Santrock, Florin Selagea, and Robert Sommer. *Self-Help That Works: Resources to Improve Emotional Health and Strengthen Relationships*, 162, 165. New York: Oxford University Press, 2013.

Porzig-Drummond, Renata, Richard J. Stevenson, and Carol Stevenson. "The 1-2-3 Magic Parenting Program and Its Effect on Child Problem Behaviors and Dysfunctional Parenting: A Randomized Controlled Trial." *Behaviour Research and Therapy* 58C (May 2014): 52–64. doi: 10.1016/j.brat.2014.05.004.

Salehpour, Yeganeh. "1-2-3 Magic Part I: Its Effectiveness on Parental Function in Child Discipline with Preschool Children." Abstract. *Dissertation Abstracts International*, Section A: Humanities & Social Sciences 57, no 3-A (September 1996): 1009.

Tutty, Steve, Harlan Gephart, and Katie Wurzbacher. "Enhancing Behavioral and Social Skill Functioning in Children Newly Diagnosed with Attention Deficit Hyperactivity Disorder in a Pediatric Setting." *Developmental and Behavioral Pediatrics* 24, no.1 (February 2003): 51–57.

INDEX

A

ADHD (attention deficit/
hyperactivity disorder)
artificial reinforcers with, 155
counting method with, 32–33,
63
homework strategies, 191, 192,
194
ignoring messy bedrooms, 175
intimidation testing tactic, 114
adolescents, 18, 163, 248
affection, as testing tactic, 117
aggressive pouting, 95
allowance. See docking system
anger. See intimidation (temper)
testing tactic; parental anger;
temper tantrums
anxiety, 175
during BreakTime (or rest
period), 50
counting modification for
special needs children, 63
dropping off child at day care,
61–62, 217
"Anxious Parent, Angry Child"
syndrome, 240
apologies, 62, 117
arguing. See Little Adult
Assumption; No Talking
and No Emotion Rules;
sibling rivalry; testing and
manipulation
artificial reinforcers, 154
for cleaning up and chores, 177,
180
definition and use of, 155–157
examples of, 156–157
for homework, 194
assignment sheets/notebooks
for homework, 191
attention deficit/hyperactivity
disorder. See ADHD

authority, negotiating your, 38
autism spectrum disorders, 63
automatic parenting habits, 5–6

B

babysitters, xiii, 39
badgering
    basic tactics of, 113–114
    ignoring, 36
    managing, 121–123, 134–136, 177
bad words, 31
bathroom, BreakTime (or rest period) in, 59
bed, getting out of, at night, 198–200
bedrooms
    BreakTime (or rest period), use for, 29–30, 43–44, 48–50, 51–52, 57–59, 93, 130
    cleaning up, 58, 142, 176–177, 219
    messy, ignoring, 175–176
bedtime problems, 196–205
    basic strategy for, 197–198
    getting out of bed, 198–200
    mistaken use of counting for, 134
    nighttime waking, 200–202
    parental expectations about, 220–221
    real-life stories, 202–204
    staying consistent, 260
begging, parental, 33

behavioral problems. *See* 1-2-3 Magic program; Start behavior; Stop behavior
bipolar children, 114
bonding. *See* strengthening parent-child relationship
brains, adult, 14, 64–65, 75, 108, 138, 266
brains, children's, 24
    carrying out plans, 194–195
    cleaning up and chores, 181
    counting gently, but firmly, 41
    emotions and, 238
    executive functioning abilities, 162–164
    Little Adult Assumption and, 19, 221
    mealtime and, 187–188
    morning routines and, 172
    1-2-3 Magic program and, xv–xvi, 7, 14, 108
    one-on-one time with your child, 246–247
    overparenting and, 241–242
    parenting consistency and, 261–262
    parenting jobs, related to, 14
    public situations and, 75
    sibling rivalry and, 104
    sleep, importance of, 204–205
    solving problems together, 252
    Start behavior and, 162–165
    testing/manipulation tactics and, 125
    toddlers, 163, 181

Index 273

breakfast, 167, 168, 170
BreakTime (or rest period)
  activities allowed during, 51–52
  advantages of, 38–39
  anxiety during, 50
  basic concept of, 29–31
  in cars, 73–74, 99–103
  chair or stairs used for, 48
  cooling-off effect, 63–64
  counting method, use in, 29–31
  for extreme or dangerous behaviors, 30–31, 133
  hugs or reassurance after, 55
  kitchen timers for, 149
  length of, 29, 50
  No Talking and No Emotion Rules for, 31, 63–64, 68
  physical attacks while going to, 118
  in public places, 67–69
  refusal to come out from, 55
  refusal to go to, 43–44
  refusal to stay in room for, 48–50
  reverse, 44
  room wrecking during, 57–59
  for siblings sharing a room, 93, 130
  tantrum continues after, 94
  tantrum continues during, 50
  vs. time-out, xiv–xv
  urinating or throwing up during, 59
BreakTime Alternatives (BTAs), 29, 39
  for morning misbehavior, 168
  options for and use of, 40–41
  for public misbehavior, 69–70, 73
  for refusal to go to BreakTime, 44
  for sibling rivalry, 93, 130
  See also natural consequences
BreakTime Room, BreakTime Place, 67–69
bribery, 69
BTAs. *See* BreakTime Alternatives
butter up testing tactic, 116–117, 136

C
calendar, use in charting, 154–155
car, traveling in, 69–70, 73–74, 99–103, 149
caregivers, xiii, 39
CD (conduct disorder), 32–33
charting
  basic guidelines for, 154–157
  bedtime problems, 200
  chores, 180
  "Magic Point" of, 193–194
  morning routines, 167–168, 171
  school and homework problems, 63, 193–194
checks, as listening strategy, 229
child abuse, 16–17
chores, 97–98, 179–181
"chore voice," 148

church example, 72–73
cleaning up, 174–175
   bedrooms, 58, 142, 176–177, 219
   chores, 97–98, 148, 179–181
   counting for brief Start behavior, 158
   house, picking up around, 177–179
   lying about, 97–98
   parental expectations about, 219
clothes, wintertime, 153, 170
clothes-changing scenario, 159–160
coat on floor scenario, 158
cognitive shock therapy, 17
conduct disorder (CD), 32–33
consequences. *See* BreakTime; BreakTime Alternatives; natural consequences
constant requests. *See* badgering
"cornering," 96
counseling, professional, xvii–xviii
counting method
   basic technique for, 28–31
   behavior to use with, 10, 27
   benefits of, 36–40
   child's self-esteem, impact on, 60–61
   common slip-ups, 32–33, 257–262
   for different misbehaviors, 45
   explanations, appropriate times for, 31, 37, 63–64, 137
   gentle, but firm approach, 41
   husbands, involving in 1-2-3 Magic program, 64, 84–85
   vs. ignoring behavior, 36, 45–46
   Kickoff Conversation, 105–107
   vs. listening, 230–231
   No Talking and No Emotion Rules, 28, 36
   rehearsing, 105, 107
   spanking vs., 61
   with special needs children, 33, 63
   Start behavior, brief, using for, 157–159, 160
   Start behavior, mistake of using for, 12, 134
   for Stop behavior, 10, 27
   three counts, reasons for, 33, 52
   time between counts, 47
   what to expect, 123–125
   See also BreakTime; BreakTime Alternatives; counting scenarios; public situations
counting scenarios
   cars, riding in, 69–70, 73–74, 99–103, 149
   counting back, by child, 50–51
   dog teasing, 133
   extreme, dangerous, or new behaviors, 30–31, 133
   grocery store examples, 67, 68–69, 131–133
   guests, counting in front of, 52–55, 259
   interrupting, 135–136
   lying, 95–98

mealtime misbehavior, 184–185, 186
morning misbehavior, 168
phone calls, disruptions during, 55–56
possessiveness, 137
pouting, 95, 122
real-life stories, 76–90, 99–103, 127–138
school, problems at, 62–63, 96–98
sibling rivalry. *see* sibling rivalry
tantrums. *see* temper tantrums
testing and manipulation tactics, 30, 121–122, 123–124, 134–137, 151, 176–177
toilet training, 59–60
Twinkie example, 34–36
"window of opportunity" rule, 47–48
See also counting method; public situations; testing and manipulation
crying, as testing tactic, 116

D

dangerous behaviors, 30–31, 133
day care, dropping off child at, 61–62, 217
"delayed testers," 124
deliberate parenting habits, 5–6
demanding-firm parent role, 3–5, 9
depression, 63, 175

dictatorship to democracy, parenting as, 18, 248
dinnertime. *See* mealtimes
disappearing soda example, 250–251
disrespect, counting for, 36, 50–51, 230–231
divorced parents, xiii, 105
docking system, 158, 160
  basic principles of, 150–152
  for cleaning up and chores, 176, 177–178, 180
  for misbehavior in car, 73
dressing in morning. *See* morning routines

E

eating. *See* mealtimes
emotion, parental. *See* No Talking and No Emotion Rules; parental anger
emotional intelligence, 5, 111
executive functioning, 162–164
expectations, parental, 213–222
explanations. *See* Little Adult Assumption; No Talking and No Emotion Rules

F

family activities, excessive focus on, 186–187, 245
family meetings, 18, 172, 180, 249–251

feelings, reflecting, 228–229
55-gallon drum method, 179
firm parent role. *See*
    demanding-firm parent role
flattery, as manipulation tactic,
    116–117
friendly parent role. *See* warm-
    friendly parent role
friends, counting in front of,
    53
frustration tolerance, 17, 111
fun, sharing with children, 37–
    38, 243–247

G

garbage bag method, 178–179
good behavior, encouragement
    of, 8–9, 11–12
    See also Start behavior; specific
        behavior
grades, poor, 63
grandparents, xiii, 39, 54–55
grocery store examples, 67, 68–
    69, 71–72, 131–133
guests, counting in front of,
    52–55, 259
guilt, parental, 95, 116, 120–
    121, 260

H

hanging up coat scenario, 158
health, physical and mental,
    xiii–xiv, xvii–xviii

holding breath, as testing tactic,
    116
homework, 189–195
    capacity for independently
        working on, by age, 162–163
    lying about, 96–98
    parental expectations about,
        220
    poor grades, dealing with, 63
    spontaneous requests, avoiding,
        190
    strategies for, 155, 190–194
house cleaning. *See* cleaning up
husbands, involving in 1-2-3
    Magic program, 64, 84–85

I

ignoring behaviors
    vs. counting, 36, 45–46
    messy bedrooms, 175–176
    room wrecking during
        BreakTime (or rest period),
        58
    temper tantrums, 93–94
    testing and manipulation, 122
immediate cooperators vs.
    immediate testers, 123
independence, fostering, 5,
    162–165, 229, 241, 248–
    249
interrupting, 135–136
intimidation (temper) testing
    tactic, 114, 120, 121, 134–
    137, 151

K

Kickoff Conversation, 105–107
King Louis example, 57–59
kitchen timers
    benefits and uses of, 149–150
    for cleaning up and chores, 158, 177–178
    for homework, 194
    mealtime strategies, 183–184
    for morning routines, 167–168
    non-ticking alternatives to, 194
    for simple requests, 159

L

learning disabilities, 63, 175, 191, 192, 194
leaving, parental expectations about, 215–216
"liking" your children, 4, 13, 244
listening, parental expectations about, 214–215
listening, sympathetic. *See* sympathetic listening
Little Adult Assumption, 21, 33, 43, 82–83, 132, 161
    child's developing brain and, 19, 221
    concept of, 15–20
    negative outcomes of, 16–17, 18, 151
    negotiating your authority, 38
    "shouldy" thinking, 159
    Twinkie example, 34–35
logical consequences. *See* natural consequences
lying, 95–98, 218

M

manipulation. *See* testing and manipulation
marriage, 243–244, 264–266
martyrdom, 116, 120–123, 134–137
Master of the Quick Exit, 61–62, 217
mealtimes, 86–87, 182–188
    parental expectations about, 219–220
    Picky Pete eating scenario, 182–183, 185–186
    strategies for, 183–187
meetings, family, 18, 172, 180, 249–251
meetings with child, one-on-one, 251–252
mental health evaluation and counseling, xvii–xviii
Minor But Aggravating Actions (MBAs), 45–46
modeling behavior, 6
morning routines, 166–173
    for older children, 153, 168–171
    for small children, 154, 167–168
music lessons, 152–153, 155, 195

N

naps, 217–218
natural consequences, 150, 160, 161
   basic principles of, 40–41, 152–154
   cleanup routines, 176
   homework problems, 190–191
   morning routines, 153–154, 168–171
   music lessons, 152–153, 155
   for sibling rivalry, 130
natural reinforcers, 155, 180
niceness, as manipulation tactic, 116–117
niceness, parental, 38
nighttime waking, 200–202
No Talking and No Emotion Rules, 41
   basic principles of, 21–24
   bedtime routines, 199, 201
   BreakTime (or rest period) and, 31, 63–64, 68
   cleanup routines, 176–177
   counting method, use with, 28, 32–36
   dropping off child at school, 61–62, 217
   explanations, appropriate times for, 31, 37, 63–64, 137
   explanations, repeated, avoiding, 17, 18–19
   home-school coordination, 40
   lying, dealing with, 95–96, 98
   as "magic" in 1-2-3 program, 28, 138
   morning routines, 167, 170, 171
   reasons for, 21–24
   Start behavior, dealing with, 142
   staying consistent with, 32–33, 258, 259, 261
   temper tantrums, 94, 214
   testing and manipulation tactics, 120–121, 151
   Twinkie example, 34–36

O

obnoxious behavior, controlling
   demanding-firm parent role, 9
   overview, 8, 10
   psychological evaluation and counseling, xvii–xviii
   strategies for, 11–12
   See also counting method; Stop behavior
ODD (oppositional defiant disorder), 32–33, 63
1-2-3 counting method. *See* counting method
1-2-3 Magic program, xi–xii, xix–xxi
   benefits of, 263–266
   child's developing brain and, xv–xvi, 7, 14, 108
   common slip-ups, 32–33, 257–262

involvement of both parents in, xiii, 45, 64, 84–85, 105, 264–266
"magic" in, 28, 138
parental message to child, 57
practice, need for, 138
psychological evaluation and counseling, xvii–xviii
time-out vs. BreakTime (or rest period), xiv–xv
what to expect, 123–125
one-parent, one-child activities, 187, 197, 243–247
openers, as listening strategy, 227–228
oppositional defiant disorder (ODD), 32–33, 63
over-parenting, 239–242

P

parental anger, 16–17, 21–22, 61, 120, 145, 151–152
See also No Talking and No Emotion Rules
parental begging, 33
parental expectations, 213–222
parental guilt, 95, 116, 120–121, 260
parental requests. *See* simple requests; spontaneous requests
parental tone of voice, 147–148
parenting
automatic vs. deliberate, 5–6
basic jobs of, 8–14
biggest discipline mistakes of, 21–24
demanding-firm and warm-friendly roles, 3–5, 9
dictatorship to democracy, transition from, 18, 248
1-2-3 Magic program, benefits of, 263–266
Talk-Persuade-Argue-Yell-Hit Syndrome, 16–17, 18, 21–22, 37, 61
wild animal trainer analogy, 17
See also Little Adult Assumption; No Talking and No Emotion Rules; strengthening parent-child relationship
parents, single, separated, and divorced, xiii, 105
pets, 133, 150–151, 180
phone calls, disruptions during, 55–56
physical abuse, 16–17
physical discipline, 61
physical health, xiii–xiv
physical testing tactics, 117–118, 121
piano lessons example, 152–153, 155
Picky Pete eating scenario, 182–183, 185–186
positive behavior, encouragement of, 8–9, 11–12
See also Start behavior; specific behavior

Positive-Negative-Positive
   (PNP) method, 191–192
positive reinforcement (praise),
   137, 161
   basic principles of, 144–147
   for bedtime routines, 197
   for boosting self-esteem, 146–147
   charting technique, 155, 180
   for cleaning up and chores, 176, 177–178
   for homework, 191–192
   for morning routines, 168, 171
possessiveness, 137
potty training, 59–60, 216–217
pouting, 95, 116, 122
power, as motivation for
   behavior, 22–23
praise. *See* positive
   reinforcement
preschool, dropping off child
   at, 61–62, 217
preschoolers and toddlers, 94, 143, 163, 181
promises, as manipulation
   tactic, 117
psychological evaluation and
   counseling, xvii–xviii
public situations
   badgering in, 113
   BreakTime Room, BreakTime
      Place, 67–69
   car, riding in, 69–70, 73–74, 99–103, 149
   church example, 72–73

counting in, 67
fear of embarrassment, 66–67, 132
grocery store examples, 67, 68–69, 71–72, 131–133
guests, counting in front of, 52–55, 259
if children don't want to go, 69
if children do want to go, 69–70
real-life stories, 76–90, 131–133
punishments. *See* BreakTime;
   BreakTime Alternatives;
   natural consequences

Q

questions, nonjudgmental, 228

R

real-life stories, 127–138
   bedtime problems, 202–204, 206–212
   sibling rivalry, 99–103, 127–130
   sympathetic listening, 232–237
   Temper Tantrum Terrorist, 76–90
reasoning. *See* Little Adult
   Assumption; No Talking and
   No Emotion Rules
reflecting feelings, 228–229
rehearsing counting procedure, 105, 107
rehearsing positive routines, 160–162

Index 281

relationship with children. *See* strengthening parent-child relationship
requests, constant. *See* badgering
requests, simple, 147–149, 159–160, 214–215
requests, spontaneous, 148, 149–150, 190
responsibility training for older children, 168–171
restaurant example, 76–90
rest periods. *See* BreakTime
revenge motive, 112, 120
"reverse BreakTime," 44
rewards. *See* artificial reinforcers; one-parent, one-child activities
role modeling, 6
Rough Checkouts for homework, 192
routines, for positive behavior, 141–165
   benefits of, 142–143
   rehearsing, 160–162
   strategies for, 144–160
   toddlers and, 143
   See also specific routine
running away, threats of, 115, 118, 120, 121

S

school
   dropping off child at, 61–62, 217
   misbehavior at, 62–63, 96–97
   See also homework; morning routines; teachers
self-control, 46, 162
self-esteem, 60–61, 146–147, 165, 229, 241, 263
self-punishment, as testing tactic, 116
sensory issues, 94
separation anxiety, 50, 61–62, 217
sharing, problems with, 137
shopping. *See* grocery store examples
"shouldy" thinking, 159
sibling rivalry
   apologies, insisting on, 62
   basic guidelines for handling, 91–93
   car, riding in, 69–70, 73–74, 99–103, 149
   child's developing brain and, 104
   counting method for, 91–93
   counting method for incidents not witnessed by parent, 60, 129–130
   mealtime problems, 182–183, 184, 186–187
   parental expectations about, 215
   real-life stories, 99–103, 127–130
   separating children during BreakTime (or rest period), 93, 130
   using one-on-one parent-child time to avoid, 187, 245

simple requests, 147–149, 159–160, 214–215
single parents, xiii, 105
sleep problems. *See* bedtime problems
slipping, 32–33, 257–262
spanking, 61
special needs children, 155
    counting method with, 33, 63
    homework strategies, 191, 192, 194
    ignoring messy bedrooms, 175
    intimidation testing tactic, 114
spontaneous requests, 148, 149–150, 190
Start behavior
    child's brain, functioning/ development of, 162–165
    counting, mistake of using for, 12, 134
    counting variation for, 157–159, 160
    encouraging, tactics for, 11–12, 144–160
    most aggravating problem, 174
    rehearsing routines for, 160–162
    routines, benefits of, 142–143
    vs. Stop behavior, 9–12, 141
    tips for dealing with, 141–142
    toddlers and, 143, 163
    types of, 11
stealing, 95
sticker books, 156
Stop behavior
    controlling, strategies for, 11–12

    most annoying tactic, 123
    vs. Start behavior, 9–12, 141
    tackling, before dealing with Start behavior, 141–142
    types of, 10
    See also counting method; counting scenarios
story time, 197, 260
strengthening parent-child relationship
    bedtime routines, 197, 260
    family meetings, 18, 172, 180, 249–251
    "liking" your children, 4, 13, 244
    1-2-3 method, benefits of, 37–38, 263–264
    one-on-one meetings with child, 251–252
    one-parent, one-child activities, 187, 197, 243–247
    over-parenting, avoiding, 239–242
    overview, 9, 13
    solving problems together, 248–253
    staying consistent with, 261
    sympathetic listening, 225–231
    warm-friendly parent role, 3–5, 9
    whole-family focus, problem with, 186–187, 245
suicidal threats, 115
sulking. *See* martyrdom; pouting

summaries, as listening strategy, 229
suppertime. *See* mealtimes
swearing, 31
sympathetic listening
    approaches to, 227–229
    concept of, 225–227
    counting and, 230–231
    real-life stories, 232–237

T

tactic switching, 123–124
talking. *See* Little Adult Assumption; No Talking and No Emotion Rules
Talk-Persuade-Argue-Yell-Hit Syndrome, 16–17, 18, 21–22, 37, 61
tantrums. *See* temper tantrums
teachers
    home-school coordination, 40, 62–63, 98
    use of counting by, 39–40, 47–48, 60
    See also school
teenagers, 18, 163, 248
telephone calls, disruptions during, 55–56
temper (intimidation), as testing tactic, 114, 120, 121, 134–137, 151
temper tantrums
    counting vs. ignoring, 93–94
    dropping off child at day care, 61–62, 217
    grocery store examples, 67, 68–69, 71–72, 131–133
    intimidation (temper) testing tactic, 114, 120, 121, 134–137, 151
    No Talking and No Emotion Rules, 94, 214
    parental expectations about, 214
    of parents. *see* parental anger
    physical testing tactics, 117–118
    in public places, 66–69, 131–133
    real-life stories, 76–90, 131–133
    sensory issues, 94
    starting BreakTime (or rest period) after, 94
testing and manipulation
    basic tactics of, 113–118
    counting method for, 30, 121–122, 123–124, 134–137, 151, 176–177
    ignoring, 122
    most common tactics, 122–123
    parental tone of voice, impact of, 147–149
    purpose of, 111–113, 119–121
    Start behavior, dealing with, 142
    underlying mechanics of, 118–121
threats, 115, 118, 120, 121
Three-Out-of-Four Rule for mealtimes, 185–186
throwing up during BreakTime (or rest period), 59
time-outs. *See* BreakTime
timers. *See* kitchen timers

toddlers and preschoolers, 94, 143, 163, 181
toilet training, 59–60, 216–217
Twinkie example, 34–36

U

urinating on floor during BreakTime (or rest period), 59

V

voice quality, 147–148
vomiting during BreakTime (or rest period), 59

W

warm-friendly parent role, 3–5, 9
whining, 123
wild animal trainer analogy, 17
"window of opportunity" rule, 47–48
wintertime dress, 153, 170

ABOUT THE AUTHOR

Photo courtesy of
Thomas W. Phelan, PhD

THOMAS W. PHELAN is an internationally renowned expert, author, and lecturer on child discipline and attention-deficit/hyperactivity disorder. A registered PhD clinical psychologist, he appears frequently on radio and TV. Dr. Phelan practices and works in the western suburbs of Chicago.

IF YOU LOVED 1-2-3 MAGIC...

*check out these other products from
Thomas W. Phelan, PhD*

1-2-3 Magic DVD
Managing Difficult Behavior in Children 2–12

More 1-2-3 Magic DVD
Encouraging Good Behavior, Independence, and Self-Esteem

Did You Know? The 1-2-3 Magic book and DVDs are also available in Spanish!

1-2-3 Magic Workbook
A user-friendly, illustrated companion to the *1-2-3 Magic* book that includes case studies, self-evaluation questions, and exercises

1-2-3 Magic in the Classroom
1-2-3 Magic for Teachers DVD
Effective Classroom Discipline Pre-K through Grade 8

1-2-3 Magic for Kids
Helping Your Children Understand the New Rules

1-2-3 Parenting with Heart
Three-Step Discipline for a Calm and Godly Household

1-2-3 Magic Starter Kit
Accessories to help you get started with the 1-2-3 Magic program

Tantrums! Book and DVD
Managing Meltdowns in Public and Private

1-2-3 Magic Teen
Communicate, Connect, and Guide Your Teen to Adulthood

Visit 123magic.com

NOTES

NOTES

NOTES

NOTES

NOTES

NOTES

NOTES

NOTES

NOTES

NOTES

NOTES

NOTES